Getting Ready to Teach Math for the New Teacher

Grade 3

by

Robyn Silbey

Published by Frank Schaffer Publications
an imprint of

McGraw Hill **Children's Publishing**

Author: Robyn Silbey
Illustrator: Corbin Hillam

 **Children's Publishing**

Published by Frank Schaffer Publications
An imprint of McGraw-Hill Children's Publishing
Copyright © 2004 McGraw-Hill Children's Publishing

Send all inquiries to:
McGraw-Hill Children's Publishing
3195 Wilson Drive NW
Grand Rapids, Michigan 49544

Getting Ready to Teach Math for the New Teacher—Grade 3
ISBN: 0-7682-2933-2

1 2 3 4 5 6 7 8 9 MAL 09 08 07 06 05 04

The *McGraw-Hill* Companies

Table of Contents

© McGraw-Hill Children's Publishing   0-7682-2933-2 *Getting Ready to Teach Math for the New Teacher*

Table of Contents

© McGraw-Hill Children's Publishing

0-7682-2933-2 *Getting Ready to Teach Math for the New Teacher*

Introduction

Getting Ready to Teach Math for the New Teacher will help you tackle your first year of teaching third-grade math. As a starting point, you are likely to receive curriculum materials from your school or school district. You also may be assigned a textbook or math program that includes lists of standards and benchmarks. This book is designed to support those materials. It is aligned to NCTM (National Council of Teachers of Mathematics) Standards. Content areas of study are separated into six strands: Numbers, Operations, Algebra, Geometry, Measurement, and Data Analysis and Probability. To learn math, a student must do math. Each strand includes hands-on, concept-building activities, reproducibles for independent practice, and assessment activities that evaluate conceptual understanding.

0-7682-2933-2 *Getting Ready to Teach Math for the New Teacher*

National Council for Teachers of Mathematics

THE NCTM is the world's largest mathematics education organization. NCTM publishes four professional journals, including *Teaching Children Mathematics and The Mathematics Teacher.* For more information go to www.nctm.org

Process standards are embedded in every activity and assessment. We use problem solving as an application of skills. We invite our students to reason through math processes and make sense of their answers. We have students represent values in a multitude of ways, from pictures and symbols to fractions and decimals. Students make connections between math content areas such as addition and multiplication, and between math and other subject areas through problem-solving applications. Finally, activities encourage the children to communicate their understanding in speaking, writing, and computation.

Children and Math

Students will begin the year at different stages of readiness, and core knowledge will vary from one individual to another. Because students have different styles and rates of learning, we have provided inclusion strategies throughout, as well as suggestions for integrated learning that can motivate and help them make real-life connections. All students benefit from a positive atmosphere.

Third-grade students will be able to understand abstract ideas and make choices about how they learn. Allow them to share suggestions with you and the class. Use activities to show math skills at work in games, sports, shopping, cooking, and scheduling. To address a variety of learning styles, we have included active and engaging activities that appeal to multiple intelligences. These can be supported by observation, demonstration, and manipulatives.

Good Advice!

Working through a single problem or two daily will keep skills fresh in a child's mind. Begin each class with a short skill review before a new skill is addressed.

0-7682-2933-2 *Getting Ready to Teach Math for the New Teacher*

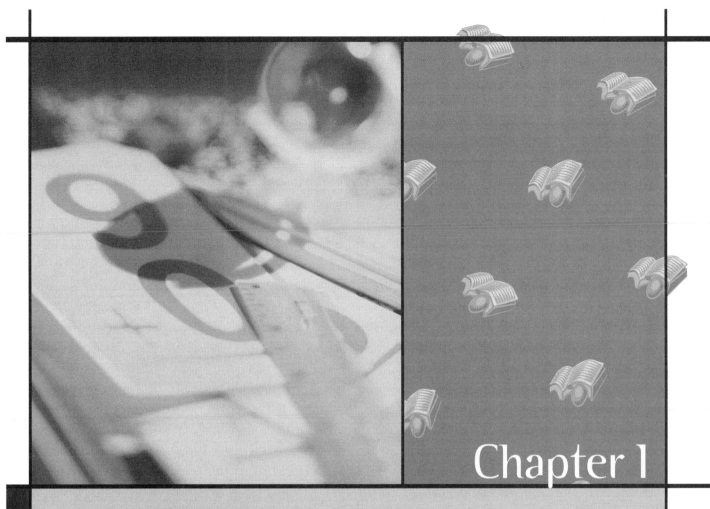

Chapter 1

Planning and Organizing: Creating a Math Environment

Long-Range Planning

Planning is essential to the success of your students. Long-range planning is the first step, with the entire school year as your time frame. Begin with the school or district's curriculum guide or course of study to ensure that students will be exposed to all required material. Use a calendar to create an overview of the year. Include special activities, holidays, short schedules, field trips, assemblies, conference times, testing times, and assessment periods. Once you have blocked out the main topics you will cover, list basic materials that you will use (such as manipulatives) that will help reinforce learning.

7

Now is the time to consider a few general classroom themes that can be fun and help to motivate students. A theme is a concept used across the curriculum to connect activities and integrate learning. Something as simple and general as holidays or seasons can work well. To provide a math connection to Halloween, students could weigh and measure a pumpkin, count the seeds inside, and decorate it with geometric shapes. Observing animal populations within a spring theme can be tied in to data analysis, probability, and statistics.

Unit Planning

A unit is a combination of activities and lessons that are based on a common topic, such as operations or algebra. Follow this sequence when planning a unit. First, determine the state or district goals to address. They are the results. You must begin with the end in mind. Next, create the assessment you will use. The assessment should be aligned with the state or district goals. Block out the time needed to teach, practice, and assess each unit. Individual lesson activities and experiences can be planned within each unit with the assessment in mind . . . so the state or district goals, the assessment, and the lessons are all aligned. It's a clear pathway to success!

Lesson Planning

You must choose, schedule, and refine the lessons that will teach each skill or concept. A lesson plan book is invaluable.

Curriculum Connections

The Teacher's Calendar (a new one every year) is a directory to holidays, historic events, and more, by Chase's Calendar of Events (McGraw-Hill/Contemporary Books, 2003). It has a special "Curriculum Connections" section that will help you put the information to use in the classroom.

Lesson Planning Strategy

A publisher's bookmap can be useful in long-range planning. On a single sheet of paper, draw one large square to represent each month of the school year. Within each square write the topics you intend to cover that month. The map can be seen at a glance. You can easily track the sequence in which each skill and concept will be taught, and you can plan to build one set of skills upon another.

0-7682-2933-2 *Getting Ready to Teach Math for the New Teacher*

Depending on your style, you can find detailed planners at teacher supply stores or online. A notebook or 3" x 5" cards can work. Your school may even supply a planner.

Learning is a continuum, and each lesson should be part of a larger picture. Begin each lesson with a bridge to previously-learned concepts by clearly stating the goal of the lesson to students. This allows them to connect new information with prior knowledge. "Yesterday/last week/last year we learned __. Today we will build on that as we learn __."

The more actively kids participate in the body of the lesson, the better they will learn. Review and reinforce at the close of the lesson: *What did you learn new today? How does this fit into what you already know?* Close with a preview of how what kids learned today will be used tomorrow.

Balance lessons by using static activities that require focus to find a particular answer or solution, activities that require creative thinking that may be resolved with a variety of responses, and activities that allow movement or hands-on participation. When planning individual lessons, consider commonplace activities that may reinforce learning. Such activities can help to balance quiet and active time. Sharing a pizza can demonstrate fractions. Baking cookies helps with measurement. Planning a party can incorporate a

Teachers Sharing with Teachers

If you would like to see how other teachers handle lessons, go to www.intime.uni.edu for a video peek.

Lesson Preparation Strategy
You should be able to explain the purpose of each lesson or activity in one sentence. Before you assign an activity, do it yourself ahead of time to identify snags. If you require materials, order or prepare them in advance. Place instructions, support material, related books, supplies, and/or pre-made copies in a plastic tub or shoe box with a cover. Label the container with the date the lesson will be given.

9

Ten Steps of Planning

- Review curriculum

- Create an overall calendar

- Block out general units

- Select general materials

- Determine state or district goals for each unit

- Create assessments for each unit

- Choose general lesson plans for each unit

- Clarify individual lessons and create a weekly/daily agenda

- Choose activities to reinforce lessons

- Review lessons to reinforce inclusive concepts

great deal of math. Your goal is to help students master a combination of concepts, facts, and skills. Be realistic about the amount of time an activity will take. Be flexible, so you can shorten or extend activities as needed. Figure in extra time to check for understanding through questioning and guided practice. If you still have a few moments left, offer independent practice.

Watch for "teachable moments" that may help you drive home a point, but return to your prepared lesson or activity as soon as possible. Remember the INPUT/OUTPUT rule of lesson planning. When the teacher provides the means for students to explore, draw conclusions, find patterns, and so forth, the students do more thinking and the bulk of the work.

Questioning

Questioning serves several purposes. It can facilitate learning, encourage classroom dialogue, and address the needs of individual students. When assessing a student, asking effective questions helps you determine what the child has learned and identify areas where he or she may still have problems.

When asking questions, use phrases that include all members of the class. Suggest that they all "think together" about an answer. Give students time to think and raise their hands before calling on an individual.

Questions that can be answered with yes/no or other one-word answers are not helpful. How or why questions encourage thinking and stimulate class discussion. Once a student has answered, you can extend and include, by asking another question or asking for peer response. When you have other students summarize the answer or address it in some way, you insure that most students will get in the habit of listening to the dialogue. This creates an atmosphere of exchange that encourages participation and, in some cases, a little risk-taking.

0-7682-2933-2 *Getting Ready to Teach Math for the New Teacher*

When helping an individual student, you can deepen his understanding of the lesson through questions. For example, if a student is working on a math story, ask strategic questions to guide him to the answer. Have the student read the information. Then ask questions such as:

What do you know?
What do you need to know?
Is there any information that you don't need?
Can you explain your thinking?
Have you seen a problem like this before?
Is there another way to think about it?
Can you give an example?
Do you see a pattern?

Your goal is to help the student understand the process, not simply get the right answer.

Questioning is an excellent opportunity for assessment. To determine if a student has truly mastered understanding, ask clear questions that require more than good recall to answer. Open-ended questions with more than one possible answer are excellent for this purpose.

Good Questions
1. *How did you solve the problem/find the answer? This gets at the process the students used to solve a problem.*
2. *How do you know your answer makes sense? This addresses math sense and reasoning.*
3. *Could you solve the problem another way? This addresses flexibility in thinking and making connections between mathematical ideas.*

0-7682-2933-2 *Getting Ready to Teach Math for the New Teacher*

Assessment Strategies

- questioning
- observation
- textbook tests
- teacher-developed tests
- rubrics
- student self-evaluation
- journal review
- portfolio review
- checklists
- conference

Assessment

The purpose of assessment is to determine what a student has learned. It is based on the curriculum, but it encompasses more. It should vary to fit the multitude of styles you are likely to find in your classroom. Formal written assessments should include multiple choice, constructed responses, and performance-based elements. The assessments in this book include a mix of these approaches. In addition to formal assessments, ongoing informal assessment should be part of everyday instruction. This includes listening to students' responses to questions and observing students at work.

At the beginning of the school year, do a baseline assessment of each student. To do this, watch students in a variety of situations, such as at lunch, on the playground, in line, in group activities, and during individual work. An early assessment should include factors such as social (communication and cooperation), behavioral (confidence and self-control), and academic (organization and work habits).

An important math assessment tool is a portfolio for each student, which can be as simple as a manila folder. Date all of the

0-7682-2933-2 *Getting Ready to Teach Math for the New Teacher*

child's math work. Allow the student access to it for review. To help with assessment, make evaluations and clip them to student worksheets. Keep the work together until the end of each report period to answer parents' questions about their child's evaluation. Make copies of any papers that highlight particular progress or concerns, and return the originals to the student to take home. Keep the most important copies on file until after the beginning of the following school year, in case the child's next teacher would like to review them.

Assessment Rubric

3   The student's performance or work sample shows a thorough understanding of the topic. Work is clearly explained with examples and/or words, all calculations are correct, and explanations reflect reasoning beyond the simplicity of the calculations.

2   The student's performance or work sample shows a good understanding of the topic. There may be some errors in calculations, but the work reflects a general knowledge of details and a reasonable understanding of mathematical ideas.

1   The student's performance or work sample shows a limited understanding of the topic. The written work does not reflect understanding of the mathematical ideas, and examples contain errors.

0   The student's performance or work sample is too weak to evaluate, or nonexistent.

Writing Assessment

Have students keep a math journal. They should write what they learned each day, how they might apply what they learned, and how it relates to what they already know. Check the journal at least once a week to see that it is up to date.

0-7682-2933-2 *Getting Ready to Teach Math for the New Teacher*

Differentiation

As you begin assessing your students, it soon becomes apparent that several levels of understanding are represented in your class. Students who cannot do the work may be frustrated, while others are bored because the material is not challenging enough. Each lesson should offer some success for every student. You may have to modify some assignments by breaking them into sections that can be completed at different rates. Include activities that address various styles of learning. When possible, offer choices for completing assignments, such as making a model or a poster. Keep in mind that every student brings special talents to the classroom.

Continuing to engage students who are having difficulty can be a challenge. Since it is your responsibility to deliver the on-grade level curriculum, you may be faced with the challenge of teaching the prerequisite skills required for success on a particular topic. For example, to add fractions with unlike denominators, students need to understand how to identify the least common denominator, find equivalent fractions for the denominator, and simplify the resulting sum. If a student cannot add fractions with unlike denominators, revisiting one or more of the above mentioned prerequisite skills may be necessary. Make time to remediate in

Women in Math

Some girls may still be getting the message that boys are better than girls in math. An Internet search using key words "women mathematicians" will provide several sites that can be inspirational to the girls in your class. Two possible sites are:

http://camel.math.ca/Women/BIOG/Biographies

http://womenshistory.about.com/cs/sciencemath/

0-7682-2933-2 *Getting Ready to Teach Math for the New Teacher*

small groups with students who are not ready to move on to new or more complex lessons. Have challenged students write short- and long-term goals for math. Celebrate reaching each goal.

When evaluating an assignment, an evaluation of 19/40 on a page of addition problems may not give the correct picture. You might consider showing two evaluations on such a paper. Put the number of problems finished over those that were not completed to show that element. Let's say 20/40. Looking at the completed problems only, put the number of correct answers over the number completed. Let's say 19/20. This gives a much better evaluation of this student.

Some students will be bored because the material is not challenging enough. These students need stimulation and more difficult material. This can take many forms. You can offer enrichment ideas, such as problem formulation or real-life problem applications of the concepts they already know. Another option is teaching a more sophisticated version of the concept. To return to the fraction example, students could add three or more fractions or add mixed numbers with unlike denominators.

Teacher Resources
Download the Help! They don't speak English Starter Kit at http://www.ael.org/page.htm?&index=58&pd=1. It is from the Institute for the Advancement of Emerging Technologies. The site offers a wealth of resources for Native American, Mexican American, and migrant students. It also addresses issues in rural education, with a special focus on mathematics achievement in rural schools.

0-7682-2933-2 *Getting Ready to Teach Math for the New Teacher*

No matter what level of understanding students may have, they will benefit from clear directions. When explaining an assignment, have students clear their desks and keep their eyes on you. Keep it simple. Tell the students what they will do and why they will do it. Demonstrate if necessary. Write the instructions on the board and have students repeat them and write them down. Answer any questions. You can even tape-record the instructions and keep the tape player on your desk for students who need to hear them again.

Tip *Celebrate Uniqueness*

To celebrate each student, create a paper treasure chest and make it the center of a bulletin board display. Learn something unique about each student and write it on a paper coin with his or her name. Perhaps a student plays chess, draws, sings, or raises guinea pigs. Pin the coins to the board around the treasure chest.

Suggested Math Period

5 minutes: Warm-up and bridge

5 minutes: Goal setting

20 minutes: Focus lesson on the day's main concept

25 minutes: Small group follow-up instruction. This may include prerequisite skills with strugglers or enriching/extending "high flyers."

5 minutes: Close and preview for tomorrow

0-7682-2933-2 *Getting Ready to Teach Math for the New Teacher*

Math Centers

Learning centers are a great way to differentiate instruction in the classroom. In addition, they promote independence and challenge students to reinforce ideas and extend learning on their own. Math centers should address a mix of formats to accommodate different learning styles. Once an instructional unit is taught, students can be invited to complete learning center activities independently to clarify concepts. Small group activities are helpful when students need additional skill practice. Centers can provide multi-level opportunities. For example, you may begin an activity at the instructional level, then enrich or extend it to address students' needs. Many of the math concepts in this book can be taught during class and the activities used for independent learning.

Math centers should include manipulatives, opportunities for critical thinking and analysis of concepts, writing prompts, games, and other activities. You don't need a lot of space to set up a center. You can keep materials and supplies in plastic see-through tubs or shoe boxes in cubbies or on shelves. Manipulatives and other small supplies may be stored in plastic bags and clipped to a clothesline with clothespins. File folders in an open-topped storage bin or box are ideal for storing reproducibles by topic. Make use of wall space with bulletin boards, instructional posters, and a magnetic whiteboard with magnetic letters and numbers.

Multiple Intelligences

- verbal-linguistic
- logical-mathematical
- visual-spatial
- bodily-kinesthetic
- musical-rhythmic
- interpersonal
- intrapersonal
- environmental-naturalist
- existentialist

Howard Gardner developed his groundbreaking theory of multiple intelligences in the early 1980s. He has since described nine ways that people may process information and learn. Most use a combination of the intelligences. Learning centers are the ideal area to address this concept. The classic math intelligence is logical-mathematical, but a student who learns through movement may be bodily-kinesthetic. An environmental-naturalist will love a lesson conducted outside involving plants or animals, while an interpersonal intelligence can benefit from peer tutoring and group work.

Making a School-to-Home Connection

Encourage parents to demonstrate to children the relevance of math in everyday life. Ask them to point out the mathematical applications when shopping, cooking, following directions, reading schedules, driving a car, etc. When parents recognize the math they use everyday and verbalize that to their children, students will see its relevance. These real-world applications help students comprehend the concepts on a personal level.

To strengthen the school-home connection, keep parents informed of the concepts students are learning in class. Send home vocabulary words and skills lists so parents can understand and help

0-7682-2933-2 *Getting Ready to Teach Math for the New Teacher*

reinforce concepts at home. Home math projects help students explore the content of their world, discover new things, organize their thinking, communicate with others, and summarize what they have learned. This allows students to become full participants and investigators in the world around them.

Avoid calling the math that students are required to do at home *homework*. Instead, use terms such as: *home challenges, daily puzzles, special questions,* or *family projects*. These assignments can be written on the board or sent home on slips of paper. Occasionally, a small prize might be given to students who, with assistance from parents, arrive at a correct answer.

School-to-Home Activity Ideas

Motivate students to explore math concepts through the use of parent-assisted projects. Follow up with activities using the projects in class.

At home:	In class:
▶ Write family recipes.	Use recipes to create dishes and/or reproduce all the favorite recipes and create a class cookbook.
▶ Cook and record outcome.	Share information and/or food.
▶ Bake desserts.	Divide a whole apple crisp into equal-sized pieces or two dozen cookies into enough parts for the whole class.
▶ Measure specifics around the house, such as number of trees in yard, length of driveways, etc.	Compare figures by creating class graphs.

0-7682-2933-2 *Getting Ready to Teach Math for the New Teacher*

At home:

▶ Record distances traveled in family car.

▶ Draw house plans or floor plans.

▶ Draw maps of the neighborhood.

▶ Check, record, and compare prices of a specific item at different markets, such as red delicious apples.

▶ Graph family-gathered data, such as favorite color, animal, etc.

In class:

Use figures to write story problems.

Draw plans for dream homes, vacation cabins, houseboats, etc.

Create a giant map of the neighborhood on a bulletin board, incorporating the figures and measurements on student maps.

Decide where to go for the best buy on a specific product.

Combine data to create new graphs.

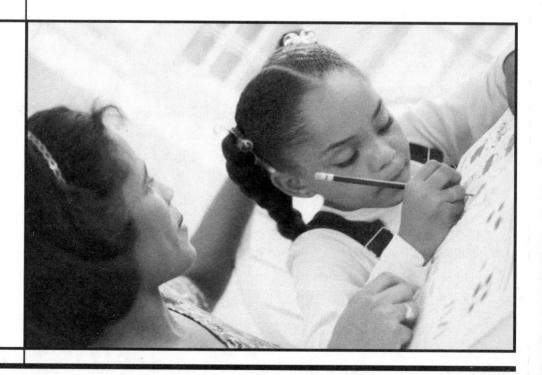

0-7682-2933-2 *Getting Ready to Teach Math for the New Teacher*

At home:

- Create time lines and family trees that include dates.

- Play card games such as "Rummy."

- Play dominoes.

- Estimate, then count large quantities, such as jelly beans in a bag.

- Compute change when shopping.

- Compute discounts in clothing stores.

In class:

Have students create time lines of their lives.

Create card games to practice math facts that can be shared during game time at home.

Make up math games that can be played with dominoes. Example: Play "War." Each player turns over a domino. The one who has the highest total keeps all the faceup dominoes.

Fill a jar with candy (pennies, marbles, shells, stones, etc.). Estimating the total might be an ongoing game. Whoever guesses correctly first or is nearest at the end of a given time period, wins the jar or another prize.

Use prices in catalogs and ads to write and solve story problems.

Use sale ads to figure discounts.

At home:

▶ Help pay the bills, estimate tips at restaurants, etc.

▶ Record patterns in nature, such as the phases of the moon.

▶ Solve challenging puzzles.

▶ Create a working sundial and/or thermometer.

▶ Build and construct kites, paper airplanes, or crafts that float.

In class:

Figure how much it costs to buy a meal ticket for a week, month, or the school year.

Keep weather graphs (rainfall, high/low temperatures, barometer readings, etc.).

Share the solutions families devised to solve puzzles.

Use devices to measure time and temperature.

Share constructions and explain the steps used in building.

0-7682-2933-2 *Getting Ready to Teach Math for the New Teacher*

Chapter 2

Number Activities

Using Manipulatives

Students need to experiment with objects in order to understand mathematical laws and properties. Using manipulatives is imperative for making the connection between a problem and the solution. Manipulatives should play an integral part in instruction in all elementary grades. A variety of manipulatives will help students grasp the meaning of math concepts and offer a fun, hands-on way of working with numbers.

0-7682-2933-2 *Getting Ready to Teach Math for the New Teacher*

Manipulatives build a student's confidence and deepen understanding because they make math more accessible. Manipulatives help abstract concepts come to life. Most math concepts should be initially explored using manipulatives.

Use manipulatives for:
- sorting and classifying (attribute blocks)
- exploring place value (tens rods and ones blocks, pennies and dimes)
- comparing fractions (fraction bars)
- measuring (rulers, meterstick, cups, pints, etc.)
- finding perimeter/area (blocks and cubes)
- exploring volume (sand and/or water center with measuring containers)

By using manipulatives, students develop a strong connection between manipulative and pictorial representation and the symbolic representation.

Manipulatives should be readily accessible to students. Children will naturally wean themselves as they gain conceptual understanding. Basic manipulatives should include:
- wooden blocks for building
- attribute blocks
- base ten materials
- connecting cubes
- pattern blocks
- geoboards and geobands
- materials for measuring length, weight, and capacity
- clocks
- fraction pieces
- play money
- learning centers—sand table, water table

**ELL
(English Language Learners)**

Invite English-learning students to compare their counting numbers with English words. Similarities will help them learn number words and reinforce number concepts and relationships, as well.

**ELL
(English Language Learners)**

The rhythmic nature of oral counting enables students learning English to acquire the number patterns more quickly. To assist them in learning, you may wish to point to the numbers on a hundred chart (page 137) as they count. This will help students associate the counting number with its numerical symbol.

0-7682-2933-2 *Getting Ready to Teach Math for the New Teacher*

Modeling Numbers with Base Ten Blocks

This activity reinforces place value and number sense concepts.

1. Have students work in pairs. Provide each pair with three number cubes and a collection of hundreds, tens, and ones blocks.

2. Player A rolls the number cubes and writes any number created by the results. Player B models the number with base ten blocks and sketches the models beneath the three-digit number. Player B writes a different number created by the same toss of the dice, and Player A models the number and sketches the blocks.

3. Players take turns until they have modeled all possible numbers. If all three dice show different numbers, six 3-digit numbers can be made.

4. Ask pairs of students to order the numbers they have modeled and write them from least to greatest.

5. Have each student write a journal entry describing what strategies he used to order the numbers.

Dollars, Dimes, and Pennies

This activity helps students see the relationship between place value and money concepts.

1. Have students work in pairs. Provide each pair with an assortment of base ten blocks, including thousands, hundreds, tens, and ones. In addition, supply each pair with ten $1-dollar bills, one $10-dollar bill, ten dimes, and ten pennies in classroom money.

2. Ask one student in each pair to represent a two-digit number using the base ten blocks.

3. Have the student's partner use money to represent the same number.

4. Ask students how the representations are similar. Help students see the quantitative connection between ones blocks and pennies and tens blocks and dimes.

5. Repeat the procedure several times, then have them use three-digit numbers. You could model an amount such as $2.19. Make sure students understand that two dollars correspond to two hundreds, since two dollars are equivalent to 100 pennies.

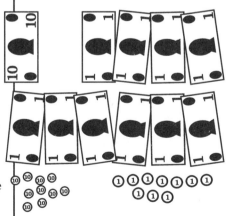

 0-7682-2933-2 *Getting Ready to Teach Math for the New Teacher*

About How Much?

Students apply what they learned about rounding numbers to round money amounts.

1. Have students work in small groups. Provide each group with a grocery store advertisement from the newspaper.

2. Tell students they will be estimating the cost of a ten-item grocery list. Make sure students understand that a healthy meal may contain meats, poultry, fish or other proteins; potatoes, pasta, rice or other carbohydrates; and green vegetables, fruits, or salad.

3. Have each group list the ten items they would like to purchase from the ad. For each item, students should record the actual price and the price rounded to the nearest dollar.

4. Discuss results as a class.

    a. What pricing patterns do students notice in the actual prices?

    b. Why is rounding helpful when finding the cost of items?

5. As an extension, challenge students to find the rounded total, as well as the actual total for their purchase.

Farm Fresh Eggs 1 Dozen 99¢

Russet Potatoes 10 lb. Bag 99¢

Sweet Oranges 5 lb. Bag 99¢

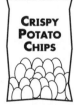

Apple Juice 64 Ounces $1.29

Crispy Potato Chips 12 oz Bag $1.79

Sauce 'N Stuff Mac 'N Cheese 16 oz Box 99¢

Snackey's Cupcakes 6 Count Package $2.29

Foamy Root Beer 6 Pack, 12 oz. Cans 99¢

Izzy's Pepperoni Pizza 14 inches $4.49

0-7682-2933-2 *Getting Ready to Teach Math for the New Teacher*

Fractional Parts of Wholes

This activity helps students develop conceptual understanding of fractional parts.

1. Distribute pattern blocks to students. Make sure each student has one hexagon, two trapezoids, three rhombi, and six equilateral triangles.

2. Tell students to think of the hexagon as one whole. Have students place trapezoids on top of the hexagon so that it is covered entirely. Ask students the following questions:

   a. How many trapezoids does it take to cover the whole? (2)

   b. What is the value of each trapezoid? ($\frac{1}{2}$)

3. Repeat the procedure for the rhombi and triangles. Students should find that three rhombi are required to cover the hexagon and the value of each rhombus is $\frac{1}{3}$. They should find that six equilateral triangles are required to cover the hexagon and the value of each triangle is $\frac{1}{6}$.

4. Once students are familiar with the fractional values of each piece, challenge them to show $\frac{2}{3}$, $\frac{5}{6}$, and $\frac{1}{2}$ using their pattern blocks.

Relating Decimals to Fractions

Students will use base ten blocks to explore the relationship between decimals and common fractions.

1. Provide small groups of students with a collection of base ten blocks. Display the hundred block and tell students that it represents one whole.

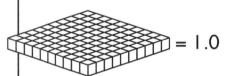

$= 1.0$

2. Display a tens block and ask students to discuss what part of the whole the block represents ($\frac{1}{10}$). If necessary, suggest that students use the tens to construct a hundred, then use what they know about fractions to determine the part represented by one tens block.

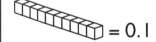

$= 0.1$

3. Write 0.3 on the board or overhead projector and ask students to model the number with blocks. Ask students to name the fractional part of the whole represented by the blocks ($\frac{3}{10}$). Have a volunteer write the fraction beside the decimal.

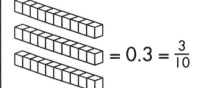

$= 0.3 = \frac{3}{10}$

4. Repeat the procedure for $\frac{7}{10}$.

5. Ask students to use blocks to model 0.5 and sketch the model. Have them write a decimal and two common fractions that can be used to represent the model. Ask each student to write a sentence or two explaining her picture and the value she recorded. (Students should draw pictures showing $\frac{5}{10}$ and write the fractions $\frac{5}{10}$ and $\frac{1}{2}$. Students should explain that 0.5, $\frac{5}{10}$, and $\frac{1}{2}$ are equivalent because they are all names for the same value or amount.)

Making Change

This activity provides crucial practice in making change. You will need a *Hundred Chart* (page 137) and coins for each student, as well as classroom items and counters.

1. Tag a classroom item, such as a pencil, with a price of 12¢. Tell students to pretend they will pay for the pencil with a quarter.

2. Tell students to cover the number 12 on their *Hundred Chart* with a counter. Explain that it represents the cost of the pencil.

3. Have students circle the number 25 and explain that it represents the amount paid, 25¢. Explain that the change can be found by counting up from 12¢ to 25¢.

4. Have students count aloud as they place three pennies (at 13¢, 14¢, and 15¢) and a dime (at 25¢) on the *Hundred Chart*. Make sure students understand that the dime represents a jump of 10, since it is worth 10¢. Students can check their work by adding the cost of the item to the amount of change received. It should equal the amount paid.

5. Repeat this procedure for several classroom items of different amounts up to $1.00.

Communication Standard

Language is as important to learning mathematics as it is to learning to read. Students must be able not only to hear and understand it, but to use the language of mathematics to express mathematical ideas precisely. In order to make assumptions and test ideas, students must be able to communicate their thoughts. Without mathematical vocabularies, students cannot do this. To optimize mathematical thinking, create and structure a mathematics-rich environment. Exploring their ideas will give your students practice in thinking coherently and communicating ideas clearly to peers, teachers, and others. Organizing and consolidating mathematical thinking through communication can be as casual as, "Friday is Jose's birthday. How many days does he have to wait to celebrate?" You will find additional strategies throughout this book.

0-7682-2933-2 *Getting Ready to Teach Math for the New Teacher*

Cross-Number Puzzle

Directions: Use the clues to complete the puzzle.

Across

A. 3,000 + 400 + 90 + 8
C. 1,000 + 200 + 60 + 7
F. One hundred thirty-five
H. Four hundred fifty-six
J. 8,000 + 200 + 40 + 1
K. Eight hundred ninety-four
L. Two hundred fifty-two
N. Thirty-two
P. 4,000 + 200 + 30 + 7
R. Three hundred five
S. Nine hundred three

Down

A. Three thousand, five hundred eight
B. 9,000 + 300 + 10 + 4
D. Two thousand forty-nine
E. Seven hundred sixteen
G. 3,000 + 100 + 20 + 3
I. 5,000 + 400 + 30
K. Eighty-two
M. 5,000 + 700 + 30 + 4
O. Two thousand, five hundred ninety
P. 400 + 9
Q. 20 + 3
R. Three hundred ninety-one

0-7682-2933-2 *Getting Ready to Teach Math for the New Teacher*

I'd Walk a Mile

Directions: Circle the letter below the greatest number. Write the letters in the blanks below. Find out how many steps you might take to walk a mile.

1.	347 M	475 N	743 O		2.	899 L	989 M	998 N

3.	789 D	897 E	879 F		4.	123 R	132 S	231 T

5.	802 H	798 I	800 J		6.	991 U	989 V	990 W

7.	8,435 Q	2,476 R	9,165 S		8.	5,032 A	4,905 B	2,480 C

9.	7,419 C	7,914 D	4,997 E		10.	6,875 S	5,092 T	6,298 U

11.	8,795 V	8,576 W	8,091 X		12.	5,689 P	5,597 Q	5,794 R

13.	4,127 H	4,190 I	4,118 J		14.	9,023 V	9,056 W	9,100 X

15.	7,904 X	7,910 Y	7,909 Z					

___ ___ ___   ___ ___   ___ ___ ___ ___ ___ ___
1   2   3   4   5   1   6   7   8   2   9

___ ___ ___ ___ ___   ___ ___ ___ ___ ___ ___ ___
10 3   11 3   2   5   6   2   9   12 3   9

___ ___ ___ ___ ___
10 13 14 4   15

0-7682-2933-2 *Getting Ready to Teach Math for the New Teacher*

Pull Apart

Directions: Look at each figure. Write the fraction for the following parts.

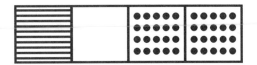

1. The total number of equal parts is _____.

   a. white _____   b. striped _____

   c. dotted _____   d. white + dotted _____

   e. white + striped + dotted _____

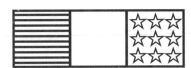

2. The total number of equal parts is _____.

   a. striped _____   b. white _____

   c. stars _____   d. striped + stars _____

   e. stars + white _____

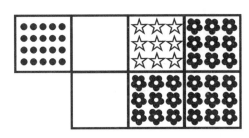

3. The total number of equal parts is _____.

   a. white _____   b. dotted _____

   c. flowers _____   d. stars _____

   e. stars + flowers _____

   f. white + dotted _____

---

4. The total number of equal parts is _____.

   a. dots _____   b. white _____

   c. flowers _____   d. white + dots _____

   e. flowers + white _____

   f. white + dots + flowers _____

    0-7682-2933-2 *Getting Ready to Teach Math for the New Teacher*

Fraction Lineup

Directions: Circle the letter below the greatest fraction in each group. Use the number line to help.

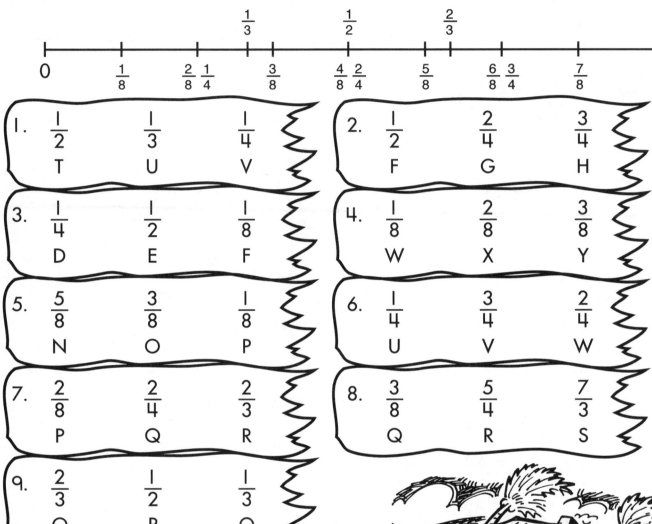

Number line: 0 $\frac{1}{8}$ $\frac{2}{8}$ $\frac{1}{4}$ $\frac{1}{3}$ $\frac{3}{8}$ $\frac{1}{2}$ $\frac{4}{8}$ $\frac{2}{4}$ $\frac{5}{8}$ $\frac{2}{3}$ $\frac{6}{8}$ $\frac{3}{4}$ $\frac{7}{8}$ 1

1. $\frac{1}{2}$ $\frac{1}{3}$ $\frac{1}{4}$
    T   U   V

2. $\frac{1}{2}$ $\frac{2}{4}$ $\frac{3}{4}$
    F   G   H

3. $\frac{1}{4}$ $\frac{1}{2}$ $\frac{1}{8}$
    D   E   F

4. $\frac{1}{8}$ $\frac{2}{8}$ $\frac{3}{8}$
    W   X   Y

5. $\frac{5}{8}$ $\frac{3}{8}$ $\frac{1}{8}$
    N   O   P

6. $\frac{1}{4}$ $\frac{3}{4}$ $\frac{2}{4}$
    U   V   W

7. $\frac{2}{8}$ $\frac{2}{4}$ $\frac{2}{3}$
    P   Q   R

8. $\frac{3}{8}$ $\frac{5}{4}$ $\frac{7}{3}$
    Q   R   S

9. $\frac{2}{3}$ $\frac{1}{2}$ $\frac{1}{3}$
    O   P   Q

Write the circled letters that match the problem numbers to solve the riddle.
Why can't hurricanes get along?

___ ___ ___ ___   ___ ___ ___ ___ ___   ___ ___ ___
1   2   3   4   5   3   6   3   7   8   3   3

___ ___ ___   ___ ___   ___ ___ ___.
3   4   3   1   9   3   4   3

    0-7682-2933-2 *Getting Ready to Teach Math for the New Teacher*

Match Made in Heaven

Directions: Use a ruler to draw a straight line from each fraction to its matching decimal.

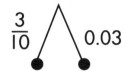 $\frac{3}{10}$ 0.03

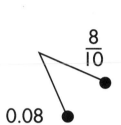 $\frac{8}{10}$ 0.08

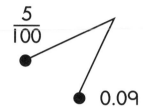 $\frac{5}{100}$ 0.09

0.05 0.5

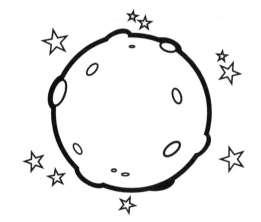

0.8 $\frac{9}{10}$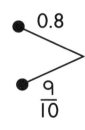

0.3 0.9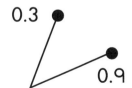

$\frac{3}{100}$ $\frac{5}{10}$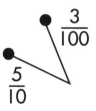

$\frac{8}{100}$ $\frac{9}{100}$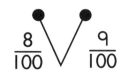

What design did you make? _____

  0-7682-2933-2 *Getting Ready to Teach Math for the New Teacher*

Leaping Along

Directions: Compare. Write < or > in the ◯ .

1. 3.7 ◯ 3.4   2.5 ◯ 2.9   4.2 ◯ 5.2

2. 6.1 ◯ 6.8   4.6 ◯ 3.6   8.9 ◯ 9.5

3. 2.8 ◯ 3.1   1.7 ◯ 1.1   4.3 ◯ 4.0

4. 3.5 ◯ 3.6   9.8 ◯ 8.9   7.3 ◯ 6.8

5. 3.1 ◯ 3.8   1.4 ◯ 2.6   3.5 ◯ 3.9

6. 4.8 ◯ 5.1   6.2 ◯ 6.5   5.7 ◯ 5.8

7. 6.3 ◯ 5.8   7.2 ◯ 7.3   8.5 ◯ 9.2

Write the decimals from least to greatest.

8.   2.3,   2.0,   2.4

9.   6.5,   6.2,   6.7

10. 5.0,   5.1,   4.9

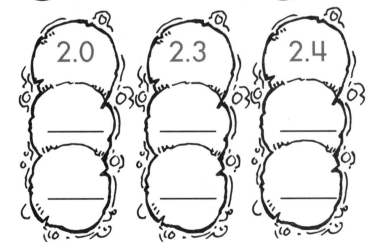

2.0   2.3   2.4

11. Describe your thinking as you ordered 5.0, 5.1, and 4.9. _____

_____

_____

0-7682-2933-2 *Getting Ready to Teach Math for the New Teacher*

Name _____   Date _____

School Store Shopping

Directions: Circle the coins that you need to get change for $1.00.
Write how much change you will get.

1. $ 0.25

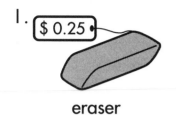
eraser

_____
change

2. $ 0.39

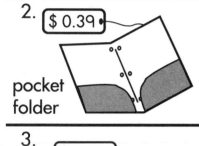
pocket
folder

_____
change

3. $ 0.55

scissors

_____
change

4. $ 0.67

lined paper

_____
change

5. $ 0.73

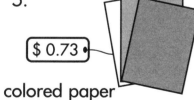
colored paper

_____
change

6. You bought an eraser. Do you have enough change to buy a pack of colored paper?

Yes   No

7. You bought scissors. Do you have enough change to buy a pocket folder?

Yes   No

35

     0-7682-2933-2 *Getting Ready to Teach Math for the New Teacher*

•Assessment•

Whole Numbers

1. Which number is shown by the blocks?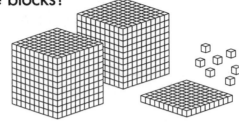

   a. 2,170   b. 2,107

   c. 1,270   d. 1,207

2. Which is the expanded form of 209,036?

   a. 200,000 + 90,000 + 300 + 6   b. 200,000 + 9,000 + 300 + 6

   c. 200,000 + 9,000 + 30 + 6   d. 200,000 + 900 + 30 + 6

3. What number is 100 greater than 5,432?

   a. 6,432   b. 5,532   c. 5,442   d. 5,433

4. 89,347 is 10,000 less than which number?

   a. 79,347   b. 89,247   c. 90,347   d. 99,347

5. Which number does NOT round to 700?

   a. 650   b. 675   c. 725   d. 751

6. Write the number for seven hundred twenty-one thousand, eighty-five. _____

7. Write the numbers in order from least to greatest.

   1,001   1,100   1,010   1,011

   _____   _____   _____   _____

8. Compare 789,101 and 788,987. Use < or >. _____   _____

9. Round 8,396 to the nearest thousand and to the nearest hundred.

   a. Thousand _____   b. Hundred _____

    0-7682-2933-2 *Getting Ready to Teach Math for the New Teacher*

Whole Numbers

10. Use the number four thousand, two hundred fifteen.

    a. Write the number in standard form. _____

    b. Write the number in expanded form.

    _____

11. Write three numbers between 1,998 and 2,005.

    _____   _____   _____

12. Describe how you would order 8,092; 7,970; 8,036;
    and 8,095. Then write the numbers from least to greatest. _____

    _____

    _____

13. The player with the most points is the winner.
    Tell who came in second place.
    Explain your thinking.

Player	Score
Carlos	4,397
Tejas	3,942
Bonita	4,808
Jen	5,003

    _____

    _____

14. Sherry rounds a number with the digits 6, 2, and 7. To the nearest hundred, the
    number rounds to 800. What is the number? Tell how you know.

    _____

    _____

    _____

15. Plot 2,184 on a number line. Tell how to round it to the nearest hundred.

    ├────┼────┼────┼────┼────┼────┼────┼────┼────┼────┤

    _____

Name _____ Date _____

Fractions and Decimals

1. What fraction of the region is shaded?

    a. $\dfrac{3}{4}$ b. $\dfrac{4}{3}$

    c. $\dfrac{3}{7}$ d. $\dfrac{4}{7}$

2. Which fraction of the group is shaded?

    a. $\dfrac{2}{5}$ b. $\dfrac{3}{5}$

    c. $\dfrac{4}{5}$ d. $\dfrac{5}{5}$

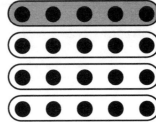

3. Which figure does not show $\dfrac{1}{2}$?

    a.   b.   c.   d.

4. Shade $\dfrac{3}{8}$ of the stars.

5. What decimal is shown by the picture? _____

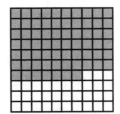

     0-7682-2933-2 *Getting Ready to Teach Math for the New Teacher*

Fractions and Decimals

6. Plot the decimals 0.2, 0.8, and 0.5 on the number line so they appear in order from least to greatest.

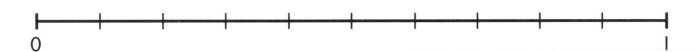

0

7. Use > or < to make the statement true. $\dfrac{3}{7}$ _____ $\dfrac{2}{7}$

8. Draw a picture to show $\dfrac{5}{6}$ of a whole.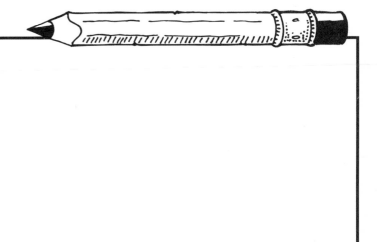

9. Draw a picture to show $\dfrac{7}{10}$ of a group.

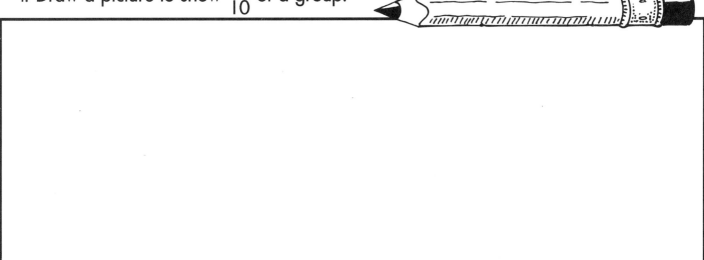

   0-7682-2933-2 *Getting Ready to Teach Math for the New Teacher*

Fractions and Decimals

10. Bill thinks that $\frac{1}{4}$ is greater than $\frac{1}{3}$ because 4 is greater than 3.

Is Bill correct? Explain your thinking. _____

_____

_____

_____

11. Write the word names for 2.05 and for 2.5.
Which is greater? Tell why. _____

_____

_____

_____

12. Write a decimal equivalent to $\frac{1}{2}$. Explain your thinking. _____

_____

_____

_____

13. Inez bought a magazine for $3.45. What change did she get from a $5.00 bill?
Draw pictures to show your thinking. Tell why your answer makes sense.

_____

_____

Chapter 3

Operations Activities

Good Advice!

Students can use manipulatives and the traditional algorithm simultaneously when finding a sum or difference. As they model regrouping with base ten blocks, they represent the regrouped "1" or "10" in the algorithm. You may wish to have students work in pairs, with one being the "manipulator" and one being the "recorder" as they work through problems together.

Vocabulary

Have students use terms such as *addend, sum, difference, factor, product, divisor, dividend,* and *quotient* when communicating about addition, subtraction, multiplication, and division. Using these terms in class enables them to use them more readily in writing and solidifies their understanding of the operations.

© McGraw-Hill Children's Publishing

0-7682-2933-2 *Getting Ready to Teach Math for the New Teacher*

Hundreds	Tens	Ones

Hundreds	Tens	Ones

Hundreds	Tens	Ones

Modeling Subtraction with Base Ten Blocks

Students will make the connection between the models and the algorithm when they complete this multi-sensory activity.

1. Provide pairs of students with hundreds, tens, and ones blocks. Have each pair of students make a three-digit place value mat for the blocks.

2. Write a math sentence such as 302 – 125 (177) on the board. Have one student in each pair model 302 with the blocks while his partner writes the math sentence on paper.

3. Have students use the blocks to complete the subtraction process, exchanging 10 tens for 1 hundred, then 10 ones for 1 ten. As the student regrouping the manipulatives completes each step, his partner should write the same step on paper.

4. Once the regrouping is finished, the blocks are removed as the written algorithm is completed.

5. Discuss the process and results as a class. Emphasize that the work with the manipulatives simply models the steps in the paper/pencil process.

6. Have students in each pair switch roles and repeat the activity for 400 – 218 (182).

Math Stories: Write and Solve

Students demonstrate their understanding of addition and subtraction concepts in this activity.

1. Provide each student with three number cubes. Have students roll the number cubes and record the greatest and smallest numbers they can make with the results. A roll of 2, 3, and 6 would result in the numbers 236 and 632.

2. Have each student create two math stories with the numbers— one that uses addition and one that requires subtraction.

3. Students write corresponding number sentences and solutions for each math story.

4. Have students share their problems in small groups and challenge groupmates to solve.

"What's the Product?" Card Game

This game may be played in pairs. For each pair, you need a regular deck of cards with the face cards removed. Place the deck facedown on the table. Each student turns up a card. The first to say the product of the two cards keeps the pair. The student with the most cards at the end wins. If you prefer, the students can divide using the smaller number as the divisor. Play a variation by having students draw dominoes from a box. The students either multiply the two numbers represented on the domino or divide the smaller number into the larger one.

42

Estimate and Subtract

Have students work in pairs. Provide each pair with connecting cubes and a 0 to 9 spinner.

1. Each student spins twice to create a two-digit number. Students compare numbers and determine which is greater.

2. Students in each pair round both numbers and estimate the difference.

3. Students model the greater number with connecting cubes, then remove the smaller number of cubes to find the actual difference.

4. Extend this activity to three-digit numbers. Have students spin three times to form the numbers, round each number to the nearest hundred, and use base ten blocks to model the numbers and find the actual difference.

Multiplication Puzzles

This activity demonstrates the relationship between repeated addition, arrays, and the concept of multiplication.

1. Provide each student with a blank sheet of paper and a pair of scissors.

2. Have students make four-piece puzzles out of the sheets by making two cuts.

3. Have students record equivalent expressions for one multiplication fact, such as 4 x 3, on each piece as follows:

    a. A repeated addition sentence, such as 3 + 3 + 3 + 3 = 12.

    b. An array showing the addition sentence, such as 4 rows of 3.

    c. A verbal description, such as *4 groups, each with 3 things, equals 12.*

    d. A multiplication sentence corresponding to the addition sentence, array, and verbal description. Here, it would be 4 x 3 = 12.

4. Have students glue the four puzzle pieces together onto a sheet of construction paper. Display finished products around the classroom.

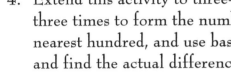

The Commutative Property of Multiplication

Students use drawings to model and increase their understanding of the Commutative Property of Multiplication.

1. Give each student two number cubes and blank paper.

2. Have students roll the number cubes twice to form multiplication facts. (Note: You may wish to have students roll again if their results are 10 or greater.)

3. Have students draw arrays showing the two factors that they rolled. For example, if a student rolls a 7 and an 8, she draws seven rows of eight objects.

4. Along one side of the drawing, the student writes a multiplication sentence that describes her picture.

5. Students turn their papers 90° and write the "turnaround" multiplication sentence that describes the picture once it is turned (i.e., reverse the factors).

Multiplication Concentration

Students learn multiplication facts as they make and play this game.

1. Have students work in pairs. Provide each pair with 24 index cards. Each student makes six pairs of cards by writing a multiplication fact, such as 7 x 3, on one card and its product (21) on another.

2. When cards are completed, have the pairs of students shuffle and arrange the cards facedown in rows between them to form a "concentration" game board.

3. Students take turns flipping over two cards. If they match, the student keeps the pair and plays again. If not, he turns the cards face down.

4. When all cards have been paired and the board has been cleared, players count their cards. The player with the greater number of cards wins the round.

Flip-Over Factors

Partners write sentences and draw pictures in a game format to make this activity fun.

1. Have students work in pairs. Provide each pair with index cards numbered 1 through 12. Students place the cards facedown. One student takes a card and draws a picture that shows that number multiplied by two.

2. The student's partner writes a multiplication sentence for the picture. She can count by twos to check the product.

3. Students can repeat this activity with any given number as the factor to be multiplied by the number on the card.

Multiplying with Base Ten Blocks

Students will use base ten blocks to model and solve multiplication facts.

1. Have students work in pairs. Provide each pair with a collection of base ten blocks and a three-section spinner labeled 2, 3, and 4.

2. One student writes a two-digit number between 12 and 25. The student's partner spins the spinner to find the number of times the two-digit number will be modeled and multiplied.

3. One student models blocks to show the equation, while the other writes it on paper. Students should combine ones and tens, regrouping if necessary, to create the product of the factors. The recorder writes the product.

4. Have students switch roles and repeat the activity.

© McGraw-Hill Children's Publishing   0-7682-2933-2 *Getting Ready to Teach Math for the New Teacher*

Relating Multiplication and Division

This whole-class activity models the relationship between multiplication and division.

1. Have a group of 12 students stand at the front of the room. Ask them to arrange themselves so that there are two groups of six students.

2. Ask the seated students to name a multiplication fact modeled by the students at the front of the room ($2 \times 6 = 12$).

3. Tell the standing students to form one group again. Ask the seated students to tell how many are in front of the room (12). Instruct the standing students to separate into two equal groups. Ask the seated students to tell how many are in each group (6).

4. Ask a volunteer to provide a division sentence that describes the arrangement of the standing students ($12 \div 2 = 6$).

5. Repeat steps 3 and 4 for three groups of four students ($3 \times 4 = 12$ and $12 \div 4 = 3$).

6. Have students write journal entries explaining how multiplication and division are related, based on the above activity. Suggest that students use related multiplication and division sentences to "illustrate" their explanations.

0-7682-2933-2 *Getting Ready to Teach Math for the New Teacher*

Dividend, Divisor, Quotient

Students learn about divisors, dividends, and quotients in this activity.

1. Have students work in pairs. Provide each pair with 24 counters. One student in each pair arranges the counters in equal rows and tells the number of rows and the number of counters in each row. The student's partner writes a division sentence based on the arrangement of the counters. The second student also completes a table, as shown, to identify the dividend, divisor, and quotient.

Dividend	Divisor	Quotient
24	4	6

2. Have the students in each pair switch roles and repeat the activity.

3. The activity continues until students have found all possible arrangements for 24 counters. Challenge students to find six different division sentences ($24 \div 4 = 6$; $24 \div 6 = 4$; $24 \div 8 = 3$; $24 \div 3 = 8$; $24 \div 2 = 12$; $24 \div 12 = 2$).

4. Discuss the findings as a class. Ask volunteers to give the dividend, divisor, and quotient for each division sentence they wrote.

Field Trip

Take a math tour of the school. Have the class visit the office, cafeteria, library, and playground. In each area, ask people who work there to name one or two ways they use math daily in their jobs.

When they return to the classroom, ask each student to list six or more ways people at school use math on the job.

© McGraw-Hill Children's Publishing   0-7682-2933-2 *Getting Ready to Teach Math for the New Teacher*

Using Base Ten Blocks to Divide

Students develop their conceptual understanding of division by working through the process with base ten blocks.

1. Have students work in pairs. Distribute base ten blocks to each pair. Have one student in each pair act as "builder," using the blocks, and the student's partner as "recorder," writing the process on paper.

2. To model and record 74 ÷ 3:

   a. The builder shows 7 tens and 4 ones. The recorder writes the division sentence ($3\overline{)74}$).

   b. The builder draws three circles to represent three sets.

   c. The builder distributes 2 tens to each of the three sets. The recorder writes 2 above the tens place of the quotient, and 6, the product of the three sets of 2 tens, in the tens place below the 7.

   d. The builder regroups the last ten as 10 ones and combines them with the 4 ones for a total of 14 ones. The recorder subtracts 6 tens from 7 tens, writes 1 in the tens place, and "brings down" the 4 ones to show 14.

   e. The builder distributes 14 ones evenly to the three sets. The recorder writes 4 above the ones place of the quotient, and 12, the product of 4 and 3, below the 14.

   f. The recorder subtracts and writes 2 as the remainder.

   g. The builder and recorder find a quotient of 24 with a remainder of 2, or 24 R2.

3. Have the students in each pair switch roles and repeat the process for 37 ÷ 2 (18 R1).

$$
\begin{array}{r}
24\ R2 \\
3\overline{)74} \\
-6 \\
\hline
14 \\
-12 \\
\hline
2
\end{array}
$$

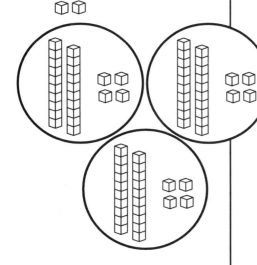

0-7682-2933-2 *Getting Ready to Teach Math for the New Teacher*

Fact Family Posters

In this activity, students combine artwork and math to show fact families.

1. Distribute a 9" x 12" piece of lightly-colored construction paper to each student.

2. Give each student a different set of numbers to be used to create a basic fact family. One student may receive 4, 6, and 24 while another student works with 5, 8, and 40.

3. Students draw arrays that show their families. (For 4, 6, and 24, a student might draw four rows of six stars or counters.) Beside their arrays, students write the four facts that make up their fact families.

4. After checking the accuracy of each fact family, have students make posters that show the fact family pictures and number sentences.

5. Display posters on a bulletin board so students can view each other's work and practice their facts.

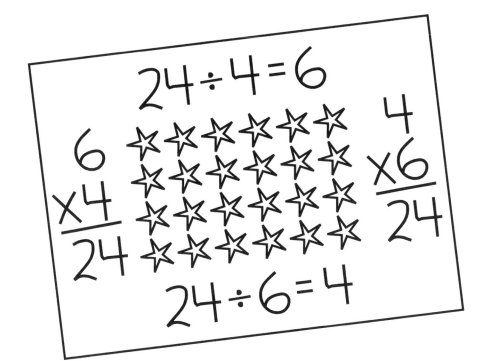

© McGraw-Hill Children's Publishing   0-7682-2933-2 *Getting Ready to Teach Math for the New Teacher*

Color by Sum

Directions: Add. Color.

847	850	892	902
red	orange	yellow	purple

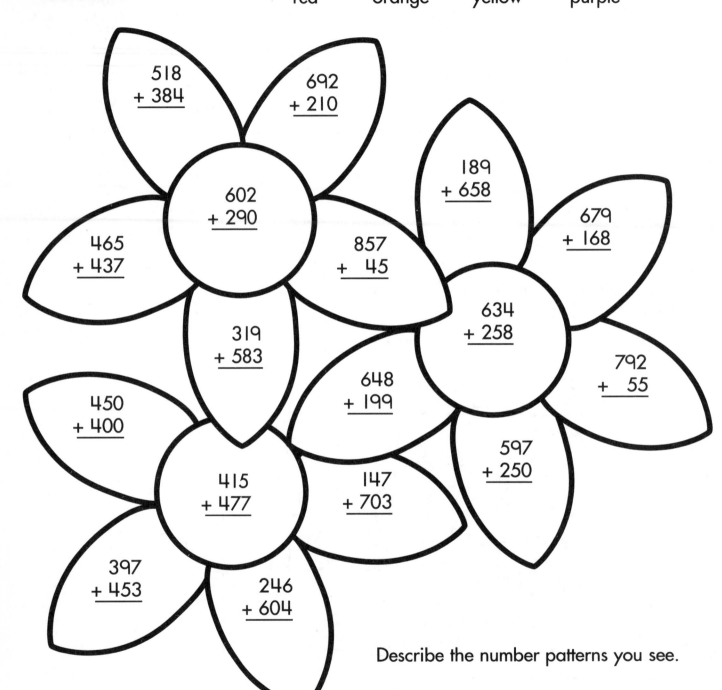

518
+ 384

692
+ 210

189
+ 658

679
+ 168

602
+ 290

465
+ 437

857
+ 45

634
+ 258

792
+ 55

319
+ 583

450
+ 400

648
+ 199

415
+ 477

147
+ 703

597
+ 250

397
+ 453

246
+ 604

Describe the number patterns you see.

_____

_____

_____

0-7682-2933-2 *Getting Ready to Teach Math for the New Teacher*

Name _____ Date _____

Nines Are Fine

Directions: Help the ant get to the picnic. Complete the problems and shade each box that has a 9 in the answer. Draw a path to connect all shaded boxes.

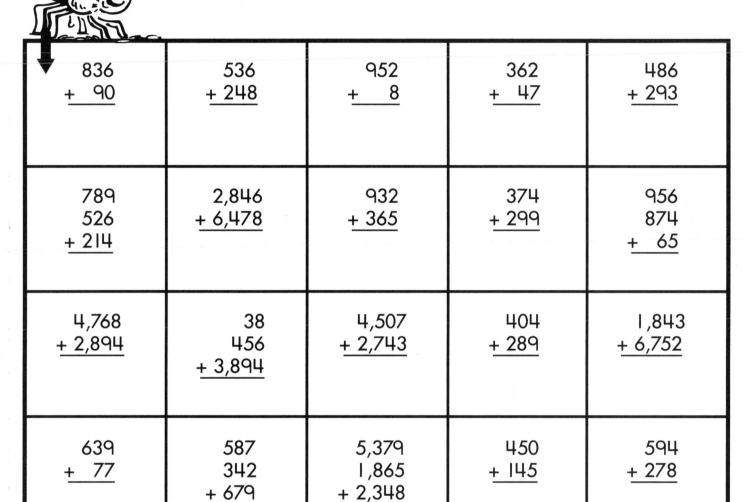

836 + 90	536 + 248	952 + 8	362 + 47	486 + 293
789 526 + 214	2,846 + 6,478	932 + 365	374 + 299	956 874 + 65
4,768 + 2,894	38 456 + 3,894	4,507 + 2,743	404 + 289	1,843 + 6,752
639 + 77	587 342 + 679	5,379 1,865 + 2,348	450 + 145	594 + 278
29 875 + 2,341	387 29 + 5,614	462 379 + 248		

Technology Tip: Check your answers with a calculator. Correct any mistakes by adding again.

   0-7682-2933-2 *Getting Ready to Teach Math for the New Teacher*

M-A-T-H-O

Directions: Subtract. Circle your answers on the M-A-T-H-O board.
Draw a line to show the winning row.

1.
```
  986        359        481        624        541
- 342      - 126      - 236      - 257      - 281
```

2.
```
  600        579        782        643        800
- 254      - 387      -  64      - 539      - 253
```

3.
```
  891        761        974        851        908
- 587      -  58      - 592      - 399      - 823
```

4.
```
  700        836        453        900        625
- 250      -  47      -  82      -  99      -  27
```

M	A	T	H	O
450	192	382	200	85
644	789	598	452	346
703	718	400	245	304
600	371	233	547	300
104	500	260	367	801

0-7682-2933-2 *Getting Ready to Teach Math for the New Teacher*

A Greenhouse

Directions: Solve each problem.

1. There are 5,460 impatiens in hanging pots and 125 impatiens in clay pots. How many impatiens are there in all?   _____

2. Sarah cut 687 long-stem red roses. Peter cut 405 long-stem pink roses. How many long-stem roses were cut altogether?   _____

3. There are 794 red geraniums in four-inch pots and 327 red geraniums in six-inch pots. How many more four-inch-pot geraniums are there than six-inch-pot geraniums?   _____

4. Mr. Wilson wants to know how many orchids are in the greenhouse. Thomas counted 386 orchids. Gina counted 974 more orchids than Thomas. How many orchids did Gina count?   _____

5. Bisu grew 3,652 pansies. He grew 1,489 fewer tulips than pansies. How many tulips did Bisu grow?   _____

6. Kevin and Emily took inventory of the daisies in the greenhouse. Kevin counted 954 daisies and Emily counted 2,187 daisies. How many more daisies did Emily count than Kevin?   _____

7. Rita waters the tiger lilies and the bachelor buttons. There are 1,254 tiger lilies and 2,741 bachelor buttons in the greenhouse. How many total flowers did Rita water?   _____

0-7682-2933-2 *Getting Ready to Teach Math for the New Teacher*

Name _____ Date _____

Catalog Shopping

Directions: Use the prices to solve each problem.

Picture Book
$2.56

Colored Pencils
$2.75

Notebook
$3.00

Ruler
$1.35

Markers
$5.47

Paper
$4.59

Crayons
$3.50

Hole Punch
$1.50

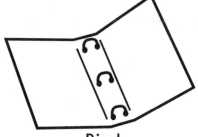
Binder
$4.85

1. How much more do the markers cost than the binder? _____

2. Sid wants to buy the crayons. He only has $1.32.
   How much more money does Sid need to buy the crayons? _____

3. Sunai ordered the ruler and colored pencils.
   How much did Sunai spend on the items? _____

4. Hal ordered the notebook and paper for
   math class. How much did Hal spend in all? _____

5. Julie has $5.00. She wants to buy the picture book.
   How much money will she have left if she buys it? _____

6. How much would it cost for Sam to buy
   both the hole punch and picture book? _____

7. Circle three items you would like to buy and find the
   total cost. Then find the change you would get from $20.00. _____

0-7682-2933-2 *Getting Ready to Teach Math for the New Teacher*

Match Game

Directions: Find each product. Match each fact on the left with one on the right that has the same factors and product. Write the letter of the matching fact. Read the letters from top to bottom to find the name for these matching sentences. The first one has been done for you.

1. 2 x 5 = __10__ __T__

2. 4 x 5 = _____ _____

3. 3 x 10 = _____ _____

4. 9 x 5 = _____ _____

5. 8 x 10 = _____ _____

6. 9 x 2 = _____ _____

7. 8 x 5 = _____ _____

8. 8 x 2 = _____ _____

9. 7 x 2 = _____ _____

10. 7 x 10 = _____ _____

11. 6 x 2 = _____ _____

12. 7 x 5 = _____ _____

13. 6 x 10 = _____ _____

14. 5 x 5 = _____ _____

15. 10 x 10 = _____ _____

A 10 x 8 = _____

A 5 x 7 = _____

C 10 x 6 = _____

D 10 x 7 = _____

F 2 x 6 = _____

N 2 x 7 = _____

N 5 x 9 = _____

O 5 x 8 = _____

R 10 x 3 = _____

R 2 x 9 = _____

S 10 x 10 = _____

T 5 x 5 = _____

T 5 x 2 = __10__

U 2 x 8 = _____

U 5 x 4 = _____

16. What are these pairs of multiplication sentences called? _____

_____

© McGraw-Hill Children's Publishing

0-7682-2933-2 *Getting Ready to Teach Math for the New Teacher*

Division Touchdowns

Directions: Arrange jersey digits in the footballs to get the correct answers.

1. 712

   $\boxed{21} \div \boxed{7} = 3$

2. 423

   $\bigcirc \div \bigcirc = 8$

3. 972

   $\bigcirc \div \bigcirc = 3$

4. 848

   $\bigcirc \div \bigcirc = 6$

5. 819

   $\bigcirc \div \bigcirc = 2$

6. 554

   $\bigcirc \div \bigcirc = 9$

7. 274

   $\bigcirc \div \bigcirc = 6$

8. 658

   $\bigcirc \div \bigcirc = 7$

9. 794

   $\bigcirc \div \bigcirc = 7$

10. 376

    $\bigcirc \div \bigcirc = 9$

11. 663

    $\bigcirc \div \bigcirc = 6$

12. 804

    $\bigcirc \div \bigcirc = 5$

0-7682-2933-2 *Getting Ready to Teach Math for the New Teacher*

Name _____ Date _____

True or False?

Directions: If the fact is true, write T. If the fact is false, write F. Then fix it.

1. $7 \times 3 = 21$ _____ $8 \times 5 = 41$ _____ $9 \times 3 = 27$ _____

2. $7 \times 0 = 0$ _____ $9 \times 7 = 67$ _____ $7 \times 7 = 51$ _____

3. $9 \times 2 = 19$ _____ $7 \times 2 = 14$ _____ $8 \times 2 = 17$ _____

4. $8 \times 9 = 72$ _____ $7 \times 4 = 29$ _____ $8 \times 0 = 0$ _____

5. $9 \times 6 = 53$ _____ $8 \times 10 = 80$ _____ $7 \times 5 = 37$ _____

6. $7 \times 6 = 43$ _____ $9 \times 8 = 73$ _____ $9 \times 5 = 45$ _____

7. $7 \times 7 = 47$ _____ $8 \times 7 = 57$ _____ $8 \times 4 = 33$ _____

8. $9 \times 0 = 9$ _____ $9 \times 9 = 83$ _____ $9 \times 10 = 19$ _____

9. $8 \times 8 = 64$ _____ $9 \times 4 = 36$ _____ $8 \times 3 = 23$ _____

10. $7 \times 8 = 56$ _____ $8 \times 6 = 47$ _____ $7 \times 9 = 69$ _____

Count the number of true and false statements.
Use <, >, or = to complete.

True statements _____ false statements.

   0-7682-2933-2 *Getting Ready to Teach Math for the New Teacher*

Multiplication Wizard

Directions: Ring answers that you predict will be greater than 700. Then multiply.

1.
$$\begin{array}{r} 351 \\ \times\ \ 2 \\ \hline 702 \end{array}$$
$$\begin{array}{r} 372 \\ \times\ \ 3 \\ \hline \end{array}$$
$$\begin{array}{r} 124 \\ \times\ \ 3 \\ \hline \end{array}$$

2.
$$\begin{array}{r} 103 \\ \times\ \ 9 \\ \hline \end{array}$$
$$\begin{array}{r} 249 \\ \times\ \ 4 \\ \hline \end{array}$$
$$\begin{array}{r} 377 \\ \times\ \ 2 \\ \hline \end{array}$$
$$\begin{array}{r} 546 \\ \times\ \ 4 \\ \hline \end{array}$$
$$\begin{array}{r} 208 \\ \times\ \ 4 \\ \hline \end{array}$$

3.
$$\begin{array}{r} 382 \\ \times\ \ 3 \\ \hline \end{array}$$
$$\begin{array}{r} 417 \\ \times\ \ 2 \\ \hline \end{array}$$
$$\begin{array}{r} 126 \\ \times\ \ 4 \\ \hline \end{array}$$
$$\begin{array}{r} 238 \\ \times\ \ 3 \\ \hline \end{array}$$
$$\begin{array}{r} 158 \\ \times\ \ 5 \\ \hline \end{array}$$

4.
$$\begin{array}{r} 206 \\ \times\ \ 3 \\ \hline \end{array}$$
$$\begin{array}{r} 324 \\ \times\ \ 3 \\ \hline \end{array}$$
$$\begin{array}{r} 168 \\ \times\ \ 4 \\ \hline \end{array}$$
$$\begin{array}{r} 295 \\ \times\ \ 3 \\ \hline \end{array}$$
$$\begin{array}{r} 128 \\ \times\ \ 3 \\ \hline \end{array}$$

5.
$$\begin{array}{r} 135 \\ \times\ \ 4 \\ \hline \end{array}$$
$$\begin{array}{r} 175 \\ \times\ \ 5 \\ \hline \end{array}$$
$$\begin{array}{r} 309 \\ \times\ \ 2 \\ \hline \end{array}$$
$$\begin{array}{r} 218 \\ \times\ \ 4 \\ \hline \end{array}$$
$$\begin{array}{r} 408 \\ \times\ \ 2 \\ \hline \end{array}$$

6.
$$\begin{array}{r} 196 \\ \times\ \ 4 \\ \hline \end{array}$$
$$\begin{array}{r} 319 \\ \times\ \ 2 \\ \hline \end{array}$$
$$\begin{array}{r} 256 \\ \times\ \ 3 \\ \hline \end{array}$$
$$\begin{array}{r} 165 \\ \times\ \ 4 \\ \hline \end{array}$$
$$\begin{array}{r} 127 \\ \times\ \ 6 \\ \hline \end{array}$$

7. Choose one prediction that was correct. Tell how you made your prediction.

_____

_____

0-7682-2933-2 *Getting Ready to Teach Math for the New Teacher*

The Amusement Park

Directions: Write the answers.

1. The Parkside Amusement Park has 329 rides. Each ride has 7 workers. How many workers does the amusement park have in all? _____

2. Jo rode the go-carts. They can go 123 feet per second. About how many feet can a go-cart travel in 5 seconds? _____

3. Meling rode on the Tea Cup ride 25 times in the last year. Nancy rode on the Tea Cup ride 8 times as much as Meling did. How many times did Nancy ride on the Tea Cup ride in the last year? _____

4. The amusement park has 9 kiddie rides. Each ride holds 134 children. How many children can be riding on the kiddie rides at one time? _____

5. As many as 518 people ride on the Shoot the Rapids ride each hour. How many people can ride the Shoot the Rapids ride in 5 hours? _____

6. Laura rode the Old Mine roller coaster. Its highest hill is 127 feet. Hal road the Blue Streak roller coaster. Its highest hill is six times as tall as the Old Mine roller coaster's hill. How tall is the highest hill on the Blue Streak roller coaster? _____

7. If 904 people ride on the Ferris wheel each day, how many people will ride on the Ferris wheel in a week? _____

0-7682-2933-2 *Getting Ready to Teach Math for the New Teacher*

Name _____ Date _____

Diamonds Are Forever

Directions:	Divide.

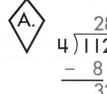
A.
```
    28
4)112
  - 8
   32
  -32
    0
```

B.
5)105

D.
3)237

E.
4)127

F.
5)150

I.
4)195

L.
3)129

N.
5)108

O.
5)206

S.
4)179

T.
3)123

U.
4)167

Fill in the correct letter over each answer.
Where can you find the largest diamond in the world?

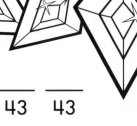

___ ___ A ___ A ___ ___ ___ A ___ ___
41R1 21R3 28   21 28 44R3 31R3 21 28 43 43

___ ___ ___ ___ ___
30 48R3 31R3 43 79

0-7682-2933-2 *Getting Ready to Teach Math for the New Teacher*

Division Check Mates

Directions: Write the answers. Draw a line from each division problem to the matching multiplication equation.

1. $3\overline{)56}$ (answer: 18)

2. $3\overline{)63}$

3. $3\overline{)276}$

4. $3\overline{)126}$

5. $3\overline{)177}$

6. $3\overline{)189}$

7. $3\overline{)246}$

8. $3\overline{)300}$

9. $3\overline{)234}$

10. $3\overline{)207}$

$$\begin{array}{r} 92 \\ \times\ 3 \\ \hline \end{array}$$

$$\begin{array}{r} 69 \\ \times\ 3 \\ \hline \end{array}$$

$$\begin{array}{r} 21 \\ \times\ 3 \\ \hline \end{array}$$

$$\begin{array}{r} 42 \\ \times\ 3 \\ \hline \end{array}$$

$$\begin{array}{r} 18 \\ \times\ 3 \\ \hline 54 \end{array}$$

$$\begin{array}{r} 100 \\ \times\ 3 \\ \hline \end{array}$$

$$\begin{array}{r} 59 \\ \times\ 3 \\ \hline \end{array}$$

$$\begin{array}{r} 63 \\ \times\ 3 \\ \hline \end{array}$$

$$\begin{array}{r} 78 \\ \times\ 3 \\ \hline \end{array}$$

$$\begin{array}{r} 82 \\ \times\ 3 \\ \hline \end{array}$$

0-7682-2933-2 *Getting Ready to Teach Math for the New Teacher*

Think About Remainders

Directions: Write the answers.

1. Ben has $14 to buy new socks. The store is selling socks for $3 a pair. How many pairs of socks can Ben buy? _____

2. There are 416 people going on a tour. There will be 9 people in each tour group. No group will be larger than 9. How many groups will be needed? _____

3. There are 365 mugs to be packed in boxes. If 8 mugs fit in one box, how many boxes are needed to package all 365 mugs? _____

4. Renee needs 3 bananas for each loaf of banana bread. How many loaves of banana bread can she make with 124 bananas? _____

5. Sue collects stamps. Each page in her stamp book displays 8 stamps. How many pages are needed to display all 79 stamps? _____

6. Linda has $26. She buys tapes for $8 each. How many tapes can she buy? _____

7. The track club is going to a meet out of town. Each van can carry 6 members of the track team. How many vans are needed to take the 75-member track club to the meet? _____

8. The drama club is having a play. Club members will serve juice for refreshments. If a bottle of juice serves 6 people, how many bottles must they buy to serve 200 people? _____

9. Choose one problem. Explain your answer and how you interpreted the remainder to find it. _____

_____

_____

0-7682-2933-2 *Getting Ready to Teach Math for the New Teacher*

Sports Center

Directions: Write the answers.

1. Ralph hung up 36 tennis rackets at Sports Center. Each hook held 6 tennis rackets. How many hooks did he fill? _____

2. Large sledding patches cost $4.79 a pack. If Gina buys 4 packages of sledding patches, how much will she spend? _____

3. A box of 12 golf balls is on sale for $7.99. If Yuri buys 7 boxes of golf balls, how many golf balls will he buy in all? _____

4. Carlos displays 81 tennis balls. They are sold in cans of 3. How many cans of tennis balls are on display? _____

5. Lee displays 275 T-shirts in 5 piles. How many T-shirts are in each pile? _____

6. Victor displays the swim goggles on 18 hooks. Each hook contains 6 swim goggles. How many swim goggles does Victor display in all? _____

7. The Sports Center sells 117 handballs in a month. It sells 3 times as many racquetballs as handballs. How many racquetballs does it sell in a month? _____

8. A new shipment of catchers' mitts arrived in 2 boxes. Each box had an equal number of mitts. If the shipment order showed 98 mitts were shipped altogether, how many mitts were in each box? _____

9. Choose one math story. Tell how you decided whether to solve using multiplication or division. _____

_____

© McGraw-Hill Children's Publishing   0-7682-2933-2 *Getting Ready to Teach Math for the New Teacher*

Shady Sums

Directions: Shade the parts to find the sum of each set of fractions.

1. ◯◯◯◯◯

$\frac{2}{5} + \frac{1}{5} =$ _____

2. ◯◯◯

$\frac{1}{3} + \frac{1}{3} =$ _____

3. ◯◯◯◯◯◯◯◯◯

$\frac{3}{10} + \frac{5}{10} =$ _____

4. ◯◯◯◯◯◯◯

$\frac{4}{8} + \frac{3}{8} =$ _____

5. ◯◯◯◯◯◯◯◯◯◯◯

$\frac{1}{12} + \frac{4}{12} =$ _____

6. ◯◯◯◯◯◯◯

$\frac{4}{7} + \frac{3}{7} =$ _____

Find the sum of each set of fractions.

7. $\frac{3}{7} + \frac{2}{7} =$ _____

8. $\frac{4}{11} + \frac{5}{11} =$ _____

9. $\frac{1}{5} + \frac{3}{5} =$ _____

10. $\frac{7}{12} + \frac{2}{12} =$ _____

11. $\frac{2}{6} + \frac{2}{6} =$ _____

12. $\frac{6}{10} + \frac{1}{10} =$ _____

13. $\frac{2}{8} + \frac{1}{8} =$ _____

14. $\frac{5}{12} + \frac{6}{12} =$ _____

0-7682-2933-2 *Getting Ready to Teach Math for the New Teacher*

What's the Difference?

Directions: Find the difference by crossing out shaded boxes.

1. $\dfrac{4}{9} - \dfrac{3}{9} =$ _____

2. $\dfrac{3}{3} - \dfrac{1}{3} =$ _____

3. $\dfrac{8}{10} - \dfrac{1}{10} =$ _____

4. $\dfrac{5}{12} - \dfrac{4}{12} =$ _____

5. $\dfrac{5}{7} - \dfrac{3}{7} =$ _____

6. $\dfrac{2}{4} - \dfrac{1}{4} =$ _____

7. $\dfrac{7}{8} - \dfrac{3}{8} =$ _____

8. $\dfrac{4}{5} - \dfrac{1}{5} =$ _____

Find the sum of each set of fractions.

9. $\dfrac{7}{12} - \dfrac{6}{12} =$ _____

10. $\dfrac{4}{7} - \dfrac{1}{7} =$ _____

11. $\dfrac{6}{7} - \dfrac{2}{7} =$ _____

12. $\dfrac{5}{11} - \dfrac{3}{11} =$ _____

13. $\dfrac{3}{8} - \dfrac{1}{8} =$ _____

14. $\dfrac{3}{6} - \dfrac{2}{6} =$ _____

15. $\dfrac{6}{10} - \dfrac{1}{10} =$ _____

16. $\dfrac{5}{8} - \dfrac{1}{8} =$ _____

0-7682-2933-2 *Getting Ready to Teach Math for the New Teacher*

Word to the Wise

Directions: Add or subtract.
Color sections with solutions greater than or equal to 5.5.

3.6 + 1.9	8.7 − 4.2	6.5 − 0.9	2.45 + 3.04	8.9 − 2.4
1.25 + 4.40	7.3 − 2.0	2.79 + 3.00	0.6 + 4.4	4.2 + 1.3
1.98 + 3.53	7.86 − 2.30	4.98 + 0.60	3.52 + 1.97	9.9 − 4.4
5.2 + 0.9	8.96 − 3.81	4.9 + 1.9	2.5 + 2.7	7.3 − 1.7
4.55 + 1.00	6.8 − 1.4	7.75 − 2.25	9.31 − 4.00	3.5 + 2.1

What word do you see? _____

0-7682-2933-2 *Getting Ready to Teach Math for the New Teacher*

Name _____ Date _____

Whole Number Addition and Subtraction

1. What is the sum of 129 and 382?

   a. 411 b. 421 c. 511 d. 4011

2. Which addends have a sum greater than 6,000?

   a. 2,345 + 3,543 b. 1,891 + 4,275
   c. 2,543 + 3,345 d. 1,189 + 4,275

3. Find the difference of 438 and 97.

   a. 535 b. 461 c. 441 d. 341

4. Which number sentence is incorrect?

   a. 4,321 − 516 = 3,805 b. 4,516 − 321 = 4,195
   c. 4,321 − 615 = 3,706 d. 4,615 − 321 = 4,214

5. One adult ticket to the movies costs $8.25. A child's ticket costs $5.50. How much more expensive is the adult ticket?

   a. $13.75 b. $3.75 c. $3.25 d. $2.75

6. Benj scored 5,690 points on his pinball game. Lia scored 715 points more than Benj. What was Lia's score?

   a. 6,504 points b. 6,405 points
   c. 5,975 points d. 4,975 points

7. What is the sum of 675; 1,394; and 828? _____

8. Find 2,103 − 1,962. _____

9. Callie bought two hamburgers for $2.79 each and a bottle of water for $1.50. How much change did she receive from a $10.00 bill? _____

10. McLean School has 792 students, while Warwick School has 512 students. Rounded to the nearest hundred, about how many more students are at McLean than at Warwick? _____

 0-7682-2933-2 *Getting Ready to Teach Math for the New Teacher*

Whole Number Addition and Subtraction

11. Find the difference of 4,002 and 964.
    Then add to check your work.

12. Which sum is greater, 5,612 + 1,290 or 5,612 + 1,920?
    Tell how you know without solving. Then solve to check your answer.

    _____

    _____

    _____

13. A nursery has 771 bushes in stock. At the end of the season, there are only
    386 bushes left. Tell how you would estimate the number of bushes that are sold
    during the season.

    _____

    _____

14. Write three number pairs with a sum of 5,656. Tell how you found your answers.

    _____ + _____   _____ + _____   _____ + _____

    _____

    _____

15. You have 1,200 tokens to spend at the arcade. Choose the
    items you would like to buy. Find their total "cost" and tell
    how many tokens you will have after your purchase. Show
    all work and explain how you solved the problem.

Item	Cost
Plush animal	469
Travel game	373
Sponge football	297
Jacks and ball	188

    _____

    _____

   0-7682-2933-2 *Getting Ready to Teach Math for the New Teacher*

Multiplication and Division Facts

1. Which multiplication fact is shown on the number line?

   a. $2 \times 2 = 4$ b. $2 \times 4 = 8$ c. $4 \times 4 = 16$ d. $5 \times 4 = 20$

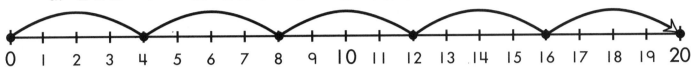

   0 1 2 3 4 5 6 7 8 9 10 11 12 13 14 15 16 17 18 19 20

2. Which multiplication fact is shown by the array?

   a. $3 \times 3 = 9$ b. $3 + 8 = 11$
   c. $3 \times 8 = 24$ d. $8 \times 8 = 64$

3. Which is the turnaround fact for 8×6?

   a. $6 + 8 = 14$ b. $6 \times 8 = 48$ c. $8 \times 6 = 48$ d. $48 \div 6 = 8$

4. Randy buys 5 packages of peanut butter cheese crackers. Each package contains 6 crackers. Which multiplication fact can be used to find how many crackers Randy buys in all?

   a. $6 \times 6 = 36$ crackers   b. $5 \times 6 = 30$ crackers
   c. $5 \times 5 = 25$ crackers   d. $5 + 6 = 11$ crackers

5. Which multiplication fact has the same product as 9×4?

   a. 8×5 b. 7×5 c. 8×6 d. 6×6

6. Write the multiplication fact shown by the repeated addition sentence.

   $7 + 7 + 7 + 7 + 7 + 7 + 7 + 7$ _____

7. What is the product of 2 and 9? _____

8. Write three multiplication facts that have the same product as 6×3.

   Tell the product. _____

   _____   _____   _____

9. Sara plants 5 rows of tomato plants with 3 tomato plants in each row.

   How many tomato plants does Sara plant? _____

Multiplication and Division Facts

10. Which division fact is shown on the number line?

   a. $3 \times 7 = 21$ b. $21 \div 3 = 18$ c. $21 - 21 = 0$ d. $21 \div 7 = 3$

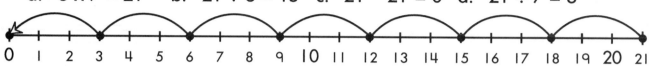

11. Which division fact is shown by the array?

   a. $13 \div 8 = 5$ b. $25 \div 5 = 5$
   c. $40 \div 5 = 8$ d. $8 \times 5 = 40$

12. Which is the turnaround fact for $32 \div 4$?

   a. $32 \div 8 = 4$ b. $4 \times 8 = 32$ c. $32 - 4 = 28$ d. $32 + 4 = 36$

13. Ethan buys a grab bag of 48 favors to fill 6 goody bags. He
    wants to put the same number of favors in each goody bag. Which
    division fact will tell how many favors will Ethan put into each bag?

   a. $48 \div 8 = 6$ favors   b. $48 \div 6 = 8$ favors
   c. $48 - 6 = 42$ favors   d. $48 + 6 = 54$ favors

14. Which division fact has the same quotient as $63 \div 7$?

   a. $27 \div 9$ b. $3 \div 3$ c. $72 \div 8$ d. $36 \div 9$

15. Write two division facts that are related to the multiplication fact $5 \times 7 = 35$.

   _____   _____

16. What is the quotient of 42 and 6? _____

17. Write three division facts that have the same quotient as $56 \div 7$.

   Tell the quotient. _____

   _____   _____   _____

0-7682-2933-2 *Getting Ready to Teach Math for the New Teacher*

Multiplication and Division Facts

18. Jacob collects baseball cards. He puts 4 cards on each page of his scrapbook. If his scrapbook contains 36 cards, how many pages are filled? _____

19. Draw an array for 6 x 7.

    Write the product. _____
    Explain how you made your array.

    _____

    _____

20. Draw a number line to show 3 x 6 = 18. Write the product. _____
    Explain how you made your number line.

    _____

    _____

21. Germaine has 12 nickels.

    a. If he trades in his nickels for pennies, how many pennies will he get? _____

    b. If he trades in his nickels for dimes, how many dimes will he get? _____

    Explain your thinking. _____

    _____

22. Write a family of facts for 7, 8, and 56.
    Draw a picture to show your family.
    Tell how all the facts are related.

    _____

    _____

 0-7682-2933-2 *Getting Ready to Teach Math for the New Teacher*

Name _____ Date _____

Whole Number Multiplication and Division

1. What is the product of 28 and 6?

   a. 168   b. 158   c. 144   d. 138

2. Which factors have a product greater than 500?

   a. 50 and 9   b. 62 and 8   c. 71 and 7   d. 85 and 6

3. Find the quotient of 87 and 4.

   a. 23   b. 22 R3   c. 21 R3   d. 21

4. Which number sentence is incorrect?

   a. 85 ÷ 5 = 17 b. 46 ÷ 7 = 8   c. 58 ÷ 2 = 29 d. 92 ÷ 4 = 23

5. A collector's crayon box contains 48 crayons.
   How many crayons are in 3 collector's boxes?

   a. 16 crayons   b. 51 crayons   c. 96 crayons   d. 144 crayons

6. Yvette and three friends shared a box of 96 markers evenly.
   How many markers did each person get?

   a. 93 markers   b. 32 markers   c. 24 markers   d. 16 markers

7. Find 157 x 8. _____

8. Find 734 ÷ 6. _____

9. Quentin mows 5 lawns and earns $28 for each one. He also earns
   $42 for an extra-large lawn. How much does Quentin earn in all? _____

10. Jackson has 234 books to pack into 9 cartons.
    How many books will he pack into each carton? _____

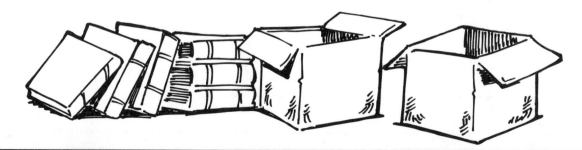

0-7682-2933-2 *Getting Ready to Teach Math for the New Teacher*

Whole Number Multiplication and Division

11. Draw pictures to show 32 x 3.

Tell the product. _____

12. Describe the step-by-step process you would use to divide 215 by 5. _____

_____

_____

_____

13. Which quotient is greater, 487 ÷ 6 or 487 ÷ 9? Tell how you know without solving. Then solve to check your answer.

_____

_____

14. Find the quotient of 618 ÷ 8.
Use multiplication to check your answer. _____

15. How can you predict whether the exact product of $74.65 x 7 is greater or less than $700?

_____

_____

_____

16. Ahmed invited some friends for dinner. He ordered 4 pizzas, each with 8 slices. Everyone ate 2 pieces of pizza, and there were no slices left over. How many people ate pizza? Tell how you solved the problem.

_____

_____

0-7682-2933-2 *Getting Ready to Teach Math for the New Teacher*

Fractions and Decimals

1. What is the sum of $\frac{3}{7} + \frac{2}{7}$?

   a. $\frac{5}{14}$ b. $\frac{6}{14}$ c. $\frac{5}{7}$ d. $\frac{6}{7}$

2. What is the difference of $\frac{7}{8}$ and $\frac{2}{8}$?

   a. $\frac{9}{8}$ b. $\frac{5}{8}$ c. 5   d. $\frac{14}{16}$

3. Which does not have a sum of 1.5?

   a. $0.7 + 0.8$ b. $0.9 + 0.6$ c. $1.0 + 0.5$ d. $1.0 + 1.5$

4. What is the difference between 1.85 and 1.80?

   a. 3.65   b. 1.85   c. 1.05   d. 0.05

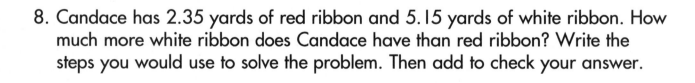

5. A new package of dog food weighs 2.75 kg. Truman eats 1.45 kg in a week. How much is left in the package? _____

6. A cup is $\frac{1}{3}$ full of water. Andrew adds another $\frac{1}{3}$ cup of juice.

   How much liquid is in the cup now? _____

7. What is the sum of $\frac{5}{12} + \frac{7}{12}$?

   Write your answer two ways. Tell why the answers are equivalent. _____

   _____

   _____

8. Candace has 2.35 yards of red ribbon and 5.15 yards of white ribbon. How much more white ribbon does Candace have than red ribbon? Write the steps you would use to solve the problem. Then add to check your answer.

   _____

   _____

9. Find the difference shown by the models below using decimals and fractions.

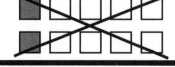 _____

    0-7682-2933-2 *Getting Ready to Teach Math for the New Teacher*

Chapter 4

Algebra Activities

Manipulatives

Students will grasp algebraic concepts more quickly if they are encouraged to use manipulatives. For example, to model a missing addend sentence, students simply use counters to model the whole, and then count out the part they know. The remaining counters represent the missing number.

Family Involvement

Encourage students to find examples of patterns at home. Tell them to look at floor tile, draperies, bed coverings, and clothing. Allow time for students to share their observations in class.

0-7682-2933-2 *Getting Ready to Teach Math for the New Teacher*

Mystery Number Game

In this game, students use clues and number sense skills to identify mystery numbers.

1. Write a three-digit number, such as 328, but don't show it to students.

2. Ask a volunteer to guess the number randomly. If the guess is incorrect, tell students whether his guess is greater than or less than your number. For example, if the student guesses 619, you would say, *The mystery number is less than 619.*

3. Ask another volunteer to guess the mystery number. If necessary, remind students that they already know whether the number is less than or greater than the last guess.

4. Continue to ask volunteers to guess the number and respond with "greater than" or "less than" clues until a student has correctly guessed the number.

5. Once students have become familiar with the rules of the game, allow them to play in small groups.

Tangram Tangler

Students apply algebra skills and their knowledge of fractions to solve these puzzles.

On the Internet

Students can find interesting information and the answers to many intriguing math questions at mathforum.org/dr.math. This is a wonderful site!

1. Have students work in groups of four. Give each student a copy of the tangram reproducible (page 139). Have students cut out the tangram pieces and place them in one large pile for their group's use.

2. Direct each group to place D pieces on top of a C piece until the C piece is covered exactly and completely. Ask the students how many D pieces are needed to make a C piece (2). Ask students what fractional part of the C piece the D piece represents ($\frac{1}{2}$). Discuss responses. Students should be able to explain that two pieces make a C piece, so D = $\frac{1}{2}$ of C.

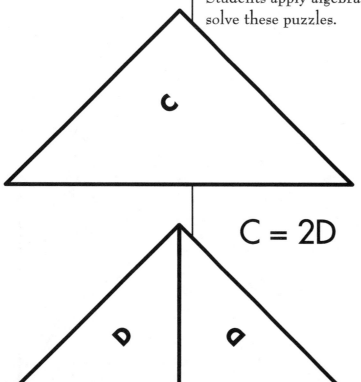

C = 2D

0-7682-2933-2 *Getting Ready to Teach Math for the New Teacher*

3. Have student groups repeat the procedure to answer the following questions:

   What is the relationship between

   a. G and B?   b. D and E?   c. G and A?
   d. D and F?   e. A and C?

   ($G = \frac{1}{2} B; D = \frac{1}{2} E; G = \frac{1}{4} A; D = \frac{1}{4} F; A = 2C$)

4. Each student should make a drawing to show the five relationships above (a through e).

Magnificent Multiples

In this activity, students use a hundred chart to discover patterns in multiples and alternative strategies for finding products.

1. Give each student a copy of the *Hundred Chart* (page 137) and pencils or markers of several colors, such as red, green, blue, brown, and purple.

2. Have students use red pencils to circle 2 and its multiples through 10 on their charts. Students should circle 2, 4, 6, 8, and 10. Continue through 20 (12, 14, 16, 18, 20). Ask students to describe the pattern they see (every other number is circled).

3. Ask students to name the seventh multiple of 2 (14). Ask students to name a corresponding multiplication sentence (7 x 2 = 14). Repeat the process for other multiples of 2 through 20.

4. Have students draw a forward slash for 3 and its multiples. Invite students to see the visual pattern this creates. (Diagonal lines from the top left to the bottom right of the chart.)

5. Ask students to name the sixth multiple of 3 and the corresponding multiplication sentence (18; 6 x 3 = 18).

6. Repeat the process for multiples of 4 and 5. For multiples of 4, have students draw a horizontal line above the number. For multiples of 5, have students draw a vertical line through the number.

7. As an extension, you may wish to have students use their multiple charts to complete sentences such as 9 x 2 = ___ x 3 = 18 (6).

0-7682-2933-2 *Getting Ready to Teach Math for the New Teacher*

Multiplication Patterns

This activity helps students model the relationship between basic facts and multiplication of two- and three-digit numbers.

1. Have students work in groups of three. Provide each group with a collection of hundreds, tens, and ones blocks and a number cube. One of the three students should have only ones blocks, one only tens blocks, and one only hundreds blocks.

2. The student with the ones blocks rolls the number cube and writes a multiplication expression by using the result with 2 as the other factor. If a 5 is rolled, the sentence would be 2 x 5. The student models 2 groups of 5 ones for a product of 10 ones, or 10.

3. If a 5 is rolled, the student with the tens blocks models 2 groups of 5 tens for a product of 10 tens, or 100.

4. If a 5 is rolled, the student with the hundreds blocks models 2 groups of 5 hundreds for a product of 10 hundreds, or 1000.

5. Encourage groups to decide how the three collections and resulting multiplication sentences are similar.

6. Have students switch blocks and repeat the activity several times.

Help for Reluctant Participants
Some students are shy about speaking up in class. If you would like all of your students to participate in question and answer exchanges, give each a 3" x 5" card. Have them write "YES" on one side and "NO" on the other. When you ask a question that can be answered with a yes or no, tell the students to raise their card with their answer facing you. If another student has answered a more complex question, the students can use the cards to show if they agree or disagree. Encourage students to explain their reasoning.

0-7682-2933-2 *Getting Ready to Teach Math for the New Teacher*

Algebra and Measurement

Tell students that they can use algebraic formulas to help them find the perimeter or area of any rectangle or square.

1. Since a square has four sides of equal length, the perimeter (p) is four times the length of one side (s). The formula is $4s = p$, where s is the length of a side and p is the perimeter around all four sides. If one side measures 5 inches, the perimeter is 4 times 5, or 20 inches.

2. Since a rectangle has two pairs of sides of equal length, the perimeter is two times the length plus two times the width, or $p = 2l + 2w$. Students can apply the distributive property to find that $p = 2(l + w)$. A rectangle 3 inches long and 5 inches wide has a perimeter of 2 (3 + 5) or 2 (8) or 16 inches.

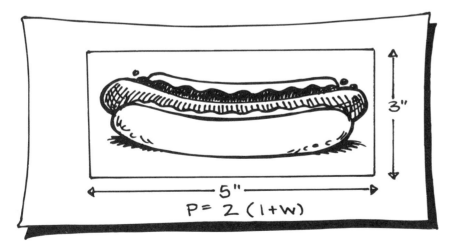

0-7682-2933-2 *Getting Ready to Teach Math for the New Teacher*

Pattern Match

Directions: Find the pattern in each row of numbers. Fill in the blanks to continue the pattern. Then match the pattern to the correct rule.

Pattern	**Rule**

1. 1, 3, 5, ___, ___, 11, 13   − 11

2. 70, ___, 50 ___, ___, 20, 10   + 12

3. 1, 8, 15, 22, ___, ___, ___   + 8

4. 36, 33, 30, ___, ___, ___, ___   − 9

5. 115, 100, 85, ___, ___, ___, ___   + 2

6. 64, 55, 46, ___, ___, ___, ___   − 10

7. 17, 25, 33, ___, ___, ___, ___   − 3

8. 96, ___, 84, 78, ___, ___, ___   − 15

9. 88, ___, 66, ___, 44, ___, ___   − 6

10. 12, 24, 36, ___, ___, ___, ___   + 7

     0-7682-2933-2 *Getting Ready to Teach Math for the New Teacher*

Nifty Number Patterns

Directions: Some numbers are missing from the chart below. Look for patterns and then fill in the chart before you answer the questions.

Hint: Which operation is this table based on (+, −, x, ÷)?

1		3			6			9	10
2	4			10			16		20
3			12			21			30
4		12			24			36	40
5	10			25			40		50
6			24			42			60
7		21			42			63	70
8	16			40			64		80
9			36			63			90
10		30			60				100

1. Circle all the odd numbers. How many squares have circles? _____

2. Put an X over the following number patterns when you find them in the grid:
   20, 27, 32, 35, 36, 35, 32, 27, 20
   5, 8, 9, 8, 5
   8, 14, 18, 20, 20, 18, 14, 8
   50, 54, 56, 56, 54, 50

3. How many squares have both a circle and an X? _____

0-7682-2933-2 *Getting Ready to Teach Math for the New Teacher*

Input-Output

1.

x	2
8	16
6	
5	
3	
9	
2	
7	
1	
4	
0	

2.

x	4
5	
2	
7	
9	
0	
6	
1	
3	
8	
4	

3.

x	7
6	
9	
1	
8	
3	
5	
0	
2	
4	
7	

4.

x	5
4	
2	
8	
3	
7	
9	
0	
6	
1	
5	

5.

x	3
7	
3	
6	
9	
2	
0	
8	
5	
1	
4	

6.

x	6
9	
3	
5	
2	
8	
6	
0	
7	
4	
1	

7.

x	8
3	
8	
4	
9	
0	
1	
7	
5	
2	
6	

8.

x	9
2	
8	
1	
4	
7	
3	
9	
6	
0	
5	

0-7682-2933-2 *Getting Ready to Teach Math for the New Teacher*

Name _____ Date _____

Division Rules!

Directions: Describe the rule in words.
Then use the rule to complete the table.

1. Rule: _____

In	5	10	15	20	25	30	35	40	45	50
Out	1	2								

2. Rule: _____

In	20	18	16	14	12	10	8	6	4	2
Out	10	9								

3. Rule: _____

In	18	15	21	9	3	30	6	12	24	27
Out	6		7		1					

4. Rule: _____

In	90	9	81	18	72	27	63	36	54	45
Out	10	1		2		3				

5. Rule: _____

In	20	40	12	32	4	24	16	36	8	28
Out		10		8	1					

6. Rule: _____

In	80	40	72	32	64	24	56	16	48	8
Out	10	5								

83

0-7682-2933-2 *Getting Ready to Teach Math for the New Teacher*

Missing Numbers

Directions: Solve to fill in the first empty square. Use that answer to fill in the square where the arrow points. Complete the puzzles.

Puzzle One

$4 \times 12 = \square$ ↓

$6 \times \square = \square$ ↓

$\square \times \square = 32$ ↓

$\square \times 9 = \square$ ↓

$6 \times \square = \square$ ↓

$3 \times \square = \square$ ↓

$9 \times \square = \square$ ↓

$\square \times \square = 14$ ↓

$\square \times 4 = \square$ ↓

$\square \times 2 = \square$

Puzzle Two

$3 \times 3 = \square$ ↓

$81 \div \square = \square$ ↓

$\square \times \square = 72$ ↓

$\square \div \square = 2$ ↓

$6 \times \square = \square$ ↓

$8 \times \square = \square$ ↓

$15 \div \square = \square$ ↓

$35 \div \square = \square$ ↓

$\square \times \square = 56$ ↓

$\square \times \square = 64$

Puzzle Three

$5 \times \square = 25$ ↓

$45 \div \square = \square$ ↓

$54 \div \square = \square$ ↓

$2 \times \square = \square$ ↓

$\square \times 4 = \square$ ↓

$\square \times \square = 21$ ↓

$\square \times \square = 28$ ↓

$\square \times 5 = \square$ ↓

$2 \times \square = \square$ ↓

$\square \div \square = 3$

0-7682-2933-2 *Getting Ready to Teach Math for the New Teacher*

Number Letters

Directions: Each problem has a letter in place of a number. Use what you know about addition and subtraction to determine the missing number.

1. $3 + m = 29$ $m =$ 26

2. $17 + 7 = a + 8$ $a =$ _____

3. $33 + 17 = s - 8$ $s =$ _____

4. $55 - 17 = t$ $t =$ _____

5. $u + 3 = 18 + 16$ $u =$ _____

6. $23 + 15 = 19 + o$ $o =$ _____

7. $b + 23 = 43$ $b =$ _____

8. $f = 27 + 46$ $f =$ _____

9. $75 - e = 30 + 5$ $e =$ _____

10. $2 + d = 49 + 5$ $d =$ _____

11. $24 = r + 1$ $r =$ _____

12. $l = 31 - 9$ $l =$ _____

13. $47 = n + 5$ $n =$ _____

14. $7 + g = 14 + 11$ $g =$ _____

15. $c = 21 - 4$ $c =$ _____

Use the answers from the problems above to fill in the letters below and reveal a message.

| 42 | 31 | 26 | 20 | 40 | 23 | | 22 | 40 | 38 | 38 | 40 | 23 | 58 |

| 52 | 19 | 42 | 38 | | 58 | 17 | 16 | 23 | 40 | | 26 | 40 |

0-7682-2933-2 *Getting Ready to Teach Math for the New Teacher*

Name _____ Date _____

Algebra

1. What are the next three numbers in the pattern? 1, 5, 9, 13, ___, ___, ___

     a. 15, 17, 19   b. 15, 19, 23   c. 17, 21, 25   d. 17, 19, 21

2. What are the next three numbers in the pattern? 1, 2, 4, 8, ___, ___, ___

     a. 10, 12, 14   b. 10, 16, 22   c. 12, 16, 20   d. 16, 32, 64

3. What are the missing numbers? 18, ___, 24, ___, 30, ___, 36

     a. 20, 26, 32   b. 21, 25, 35   c. 21, 27, 33   d. 22, 28, 34

4. Which phrase describes the pattern? 80, 40, 20, 10, 5

     a. Each number is 40 less than the number before it.
     b. Each number is 20 less than the number before it.
     c. Each number is twice the number before it.
     d. Each number is half the number before it.

5. Write a sentence to describe the pattern. 2, 12, 6, 16, 10, 20, 14

_____

6. Which shape is next in the pattern? _____

7. Which shape is next in the pattern? Draw it.

     0-7682-2933-2 *Getting Ready to Teach Math for the New Teacher*

•Assessment•

Algebra

8. What is the value of r in the equation $r + 15 = 32$?

   a. $r = 17$ b. $r = 23$ c. $r = 27$ d. $r = 47$

9. What is the value of x in the equation $x - 5 = 20$?

   a. $x = 100$ b. $x = 25$ c. $x = 15$ d. $x = 4$

10. What is the value of p in the equation $5p = 10$?

    a. $p = 5$ b. $p = 4$ c. $p = 3$ d. $p = 2$

11. A number's value is 36 when multiplied by 4. What is the number?

    a. 9   b. 40   c. 72   d. 144

12. A number divided by 3 is equal to 2. What is the number?

    a. 1   b. 3   c. 5   d. 6

13. What is the missing number? _____

    $45 - e = 39$

14. What is the missing number? _____

    $12 \div f = 3$

15. Tendall had 24 seashells left in his bucket after he gave 13 away to his sister, Tangela. How many seashells did Tendall have to begin with? _____

16. Erin has 9 toy cars. Robbie has 3 times as many toy cars as Erin. How many toy cars does Robbie have? _____

17. When a number is divided by 3, its quotient is 3 less than 7. What is the number? _____

0-7682-2933-2 *Getting Ready to Teach Math for the New Teacher*

•Assessment•
Algebra

18. What beads are missing
from the necklace?
Tell how you know.

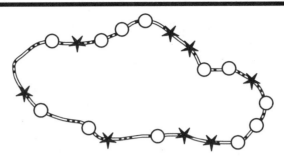

_____

_____

_____

19. Complete the function table. Write a sentence describing the rule.

Rule: _____

Input	21	49	63	14	35	72	42	28
Output	3		9			8		4

20. Complete the function table. Write a sentence describing the rule.

Rule: _____

Input	41	53	59	63	75	78	80	82
Output	32	44				69		73

21. Start with any number between 5 and 15. Double the number. Add 8.
Subtract your original number. Then subtract 4. Is the number 4 more
than the number you started with? Try the trick with another number.
Does it sill work? Will it always work? Explain your reasoning.

_____

_____

_____

  0-7682-2933-2 *Getting Ready to Teach Math for the New Teacher*

Geometry Activities

Vocabulary

Have your students reinforce geometric terms by inviting them to identify spheres, rectangular prisms, and cubes in the classroom. You also may have students classify the quadrilateral shapes they see as trapezoids, rectangles, rhombi, squares, or parallelograms.

Technology Tip

The National Council of Teachers of Mathematics is an excellent source for materials related to all math topics, including geometry. Log on to their Web site at www.nctm.org for information, teaching strategies, and other valuable information.

0-7682-2933-2 *Getting Ready to Teach Math for the New Teacher*

Congruent figures:
figures that are the
same size and shape

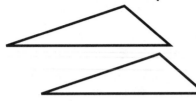

These figures are congruent.

Similar figures:
figures that are the
same shape but differ
in size

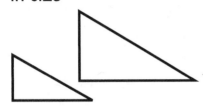

These figures are similar.

Geometry Glossary

In this activity, students make their own glossaries of geometry terms to use during this unit of study.

1. Have students create a glossary of the terms that they learn during their geometry unit. Glossaries should include definitions in students' own words and original illustrations.

2. Encourage students to make their glossary entries as thorough as possible so they can be used as reference tools in the future. Glossary terms may include, but should not be limited to, the following:

a. line   b. ray   c. line segment
d. perimeter   e. area   f. solid figure
g. face   h. edge   i. vertex
j. quadrilateral   k. polygon   l. symmetry
m. plane figure   n. congruent figures   o. similar figures
p. reflection   q. rotation

Congruent and Similar Object Hunt

Students visually explore the classroom for examples of congruent and similar figures.

1. Provide students with blank sheets of paper. Have them fold their papers in half vertically.

2. Give students five minutes to jot down any examples of congruent or similar figures they see in the classroom. Be certain students understand that all congruent figures are similar, but all similar figures are not congruent.

3. After five minutes, have students compare their lists in small groups. Encourage them to verify their hunches, if necessary, by comparing or measuring the figures.

0-7682-2933-2 *Getting Ready to Teach Math for the New Teacher*

Tangram Fun

Use tangrams to reinforce students' knowledge of geometry terms and vocabulary.

1. Give each student a copy of *Tangrams* (page 139). Ask students to identify the shape of each lettered figure. (A, C, D, F, and G are triangles; B is a parallelogram; E is a square.)

2. Ask students to name any figures in the tangram that are congruent to each other. (A and F are congruent; D and G are congruent.)

3. Ask students to name any figures in the tangram that are similar to each other. (A is similar to C, D, and G. C is similar to A, D, F, and G. D is similar to C, A, and F.)

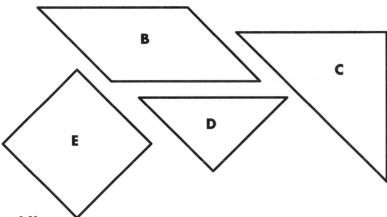

Hands On

When you introduce the concept of geometric shapes, extend it beyond visual learning. Gather items of various shapes and sizes. Include spheres, cylinders, squares, and more. Place the objects in a bag and have students take turns reaching in to feel them. Ask each student to search for a particular shape and remove it from the bag.

Plane Riddles

Have each student make up a "What Shape Am I?" riddle for one of the following plane shapes:

1. equilateral triangle (three sides, all sides same length)
2. isosceles triangle (three sides, two sides same length)
3. scalene triangle (three sides, all sides different length)
4. square (four sides, all sides same length, four right angles)
5. rectangle (four sides, two sets of parallel sides, four right angles)
6. trapezoid (four sides, one set of parallel sides)
7. parallelogram (four sides, opposite sides the same length and parallel)
8. rhombus (four sides, parallelogram with four sides same length)

When students have completed their riddles, allow them time to challenge their classmates to solve.

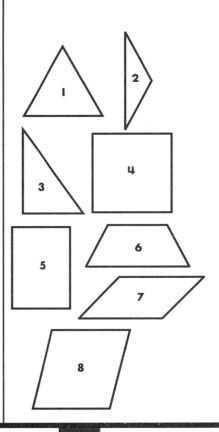

0-7682-2933-2 *Getting Ready to Teach Math for the New Teacher*

Creating Shapes

Use 24 toothpicks to make a series of nine squares in three rows. Ask students to tell you how many squares they can find. They are likely to say nine. There are in fact fourteen. Each corner is made up of four squares, and there is one large square. Using clay to join the toothpicks, have students build as many shapes as possible. They can make triangles, pyramids, squares, cubes, and more.

Exploring Perimeter and Area

These two activities help students see the relationship between perimeter and area. Provide each student with *Centimeter Grid Paper* (page 138).

1. Have students shade as many different rectangles as they can with areas of 12 square units. Students should draw rectangles 3 units wide by 4 units long, 2 units wide by 6 units long, and 12 units wide by 1 unit long. For each rectangle, have students calculate the perimeter. Then pose the following questions for discussion:

   a. *If two rectangles have the same area, will they always have the same perimeter?* (No)

   b. *Which rectangle has the smallest perimeter?* (The rectangle that is closest in shape to a square)

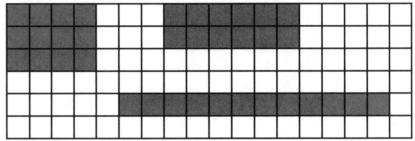

2. Have students sketch as many different rectangles as they can with perimeters of 14 units. Students should draw rectangles showing 6 by 1 units, 5 by 2 units, and 4 by 3 units. For each rectangle, have students calculate the area. Have students respond to the following questions:

   a. *If two rectangles have the same perimeter, will they always have the same area?* (No)

   b. *Which rectangle has the greatest area?* (The rectangle that is closest in shape to a square)

   c. *Which rectangle has the smallest area?* (The longest, narrowest rectangle)

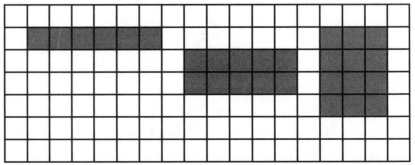

0-7682-2933-2 *Getting Ready to Teach Math for the New Teacher*

Symmetrical Words and Names

In this activity, students will find words and names that are symmetrical.

1. Have students list the letters that have vertical (A, H, I, M, O, T, U, V, W, X, Y) and horizontal (B, C, D, E, H, I, K, O, X) symmetry.

2. Challenge them to write words or names composed of all vertically or horizontally symmetrical letters. For example, the word WAX has vertical symmetry; the word CHEEK has horizontal symmetry.

3. Distribute plain paper and crayons. Have students fold the paper in half lengthwise for a word with vertical symmetry and widthwise for a word with horizontal symmetry. Have students write one half of the word along the fold line.

4. Invite students to exchange papers with a classmate to complete the design and identify the symmetrical word.

0-7682-2933-2 *Getting Ready to Teach Math for the New Teacher*

Solid Figures

Directions: Use the solid figures shown below. Count the number of faces, edges, and vertices in each figure. Record your findings in the table.

| Cube | Rectangular prism | Pyramid | Triangular pyramid | Triangular prism | Hexagonal prism |

Solid	Faces	Edges	Vertices
Cube			
Rectangular prism			
Pyramid			
Triangular pyramid			
Triangular prism			
Hexagonal prism			

Use the table to answer the questions.

1. What relationship do you see between the combined number of faces and vertices and the number of edges? _____

   _____

2. Which solid figure has 4 faces and 6 edges? _____

3. Which solid figure has 6 congruent faces?_____

4. Which solid figure has 3 pairs of congruent faces? _____

5. Write your own question for a solid listed in the table. Then write the answer.

   _____

   _____

0-7682-2933-2 *Getting Ready to Teach Math for the New Teacher*

Match Up

Directions: Match a word in the first column to a description in the second column to a picture in the third column.

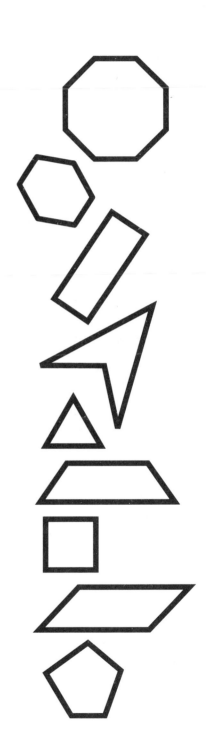

hexagon

octagon

parallelogram

pentagon

polygon

rectangle

square

trapezoid

triangle

1. closed figure that has three or more sides

2. polygon that has 4 sides and 4 vertices

3. polygon that has 8 sides and 8 vertices

4. polygon that has 3 sides and 3 vertices

5. quadrilateral that has one pair of parallel sides

6. polygon that has 5 sides and 5 vertices

7. quadrilateral with opposite sides that are parallel

8. polygon that has 6 sides and 6 vertices

9. rectangle with 4 equal sides

0-7682-2933-2 *Getting Ready to Teach Math for the New Teacher*

Dimensions

Directions: Match each three-dimensional shape with a corresponding two-dimensional shape by drawing a line. You may need to match two two-dimensional shapes to one three-dimensional shape.

1.   triangle

2.   square

3.    circle

4. 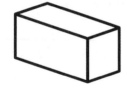   rectangle

Look at each solid. Draw the two-dimensional shapes needed to make each shape. Solids may be made of more than one two-dimensional shape.

5.

6.

7.

8. What two-dimensional object is representative of a sphere?

_____

0-7682-2933-2 *Getting Ready to Teach Math for the New Teacher*

Congruent or Similar?

Directions: Decide if the figures below are congruent or similar.
If they are congruent, color the figures yellow.
If they are similar, color the figures blue.
If they are not congruent or similar, color the figures red.

1.		
2.		
3.		
4.		
5.		

0-7682-2933-2 *Getting Ready to Teach Math for the New Teacher*

Name _____ Date _____

Symmetry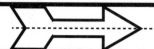

Directions: A figure that can be separated into two matching parts is symmetric. Is the dotted line a line of symmetry? Write *yes* or *no*.

    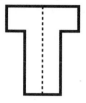

1. _____   2. _____   3. _____   4. _____

Draw a matching part to create a symmetrical figure.

              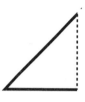

5.   6.   7.

Use letters to make symmetric words.

8. DECK

9.    10.

11. Write two more symmetrical words.

_____

0-7682-2933-2 *Getting Ready to Teach Math for the New Teacher*

Around the Rim

Directions: The distance around a figure is the perimeter.
Find the perimeter of the following figures.

1.
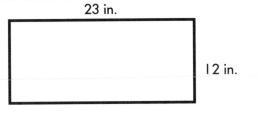
23 in.
12 in.

_____

2.
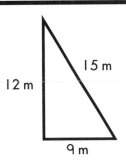
15 m
12 m
9 m

_____

3.
4 cm
12 cm
17 cm
5 cm
5 cm
9 cm

_____

4.
32 yd.
32 yd.

_____

5.
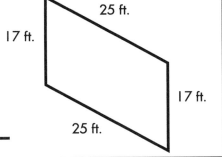
25 ft.
17 ft.
17 ft.
25 ft.

_____

6.
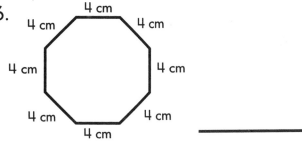
4 cm   4 cm
4 cm   4 cm
4 cm   4 cm
4 cm   4 cm

_____

7.
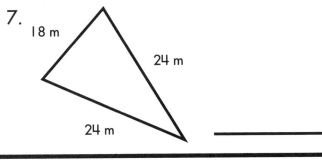
18 m
24 m
24 m

_____

8.
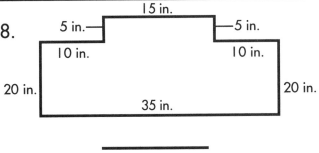
15 in.
5 in. —   — 5 in.
10 in.   10 in.
20 in.   20 in.
35 in.

_____

0-7682-2933-2 *Getting Ready to Teach Math for the New Teacher*

Calculating Area

Directions: The rule for finding the area of a rectangle is length x width. Look at each figure drawn below. Use the length and width given to find the area. Label your answer in square units. Then, find the perimeter of each figure. Label with units.

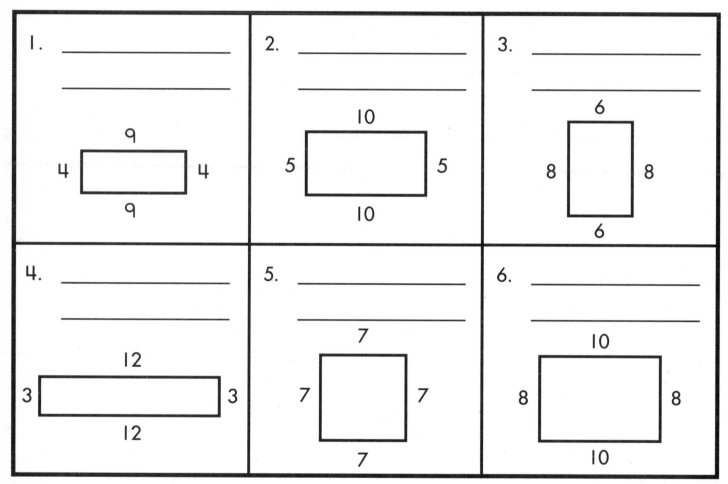

Solve.

7. Joey is covering the bottom of a wooden box with felt.
   The bottom of the box is 8 inches by 4 inches.
   How many square inches of felt does he need?

   _____

8. Tony wants to cover a trading card with clear,
   self-adhesive paper. The card is 3 inches by 5 inches.
   How many square inches of paper does he need to
   exactly cover both sides?

   _____

  0-7682-2933-2 *Getting Ready to Teach Math for the New Teacher*

Name _____ Date _____

Reflection and Rotation

Directions: For the drawings below, write *reflection* or *rotation* to describe how the figure was moved.

Reflection is one kind of symmetry. In reflection, a figure is flipped, creating a mirror image. **E Ǝ**	Rotation is another kind of symmetry. In rotation, a figure is rotated around a fixed point. **5 ഗ**

1. _____

2. _____

3. _____

4. _____

5. _____
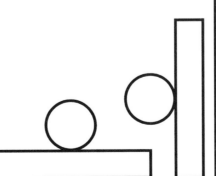

6. _____
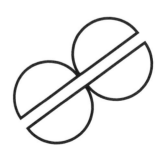

0-7682-2933-2 *Getting Ready to Teach Math for the New Teacher*

Name _____ Date _____

Geometry

1. Which shape has 4 square corners and 4 equal sides?

   a. ☐   b.  ▱   c. ▭   d.  ◇

2. Which number has vertical line symmetry?

   a. 2   b. 3   c. 8   d. 10

3. Which figure has at least one triangular face?

   a.  △   b.  △   c. 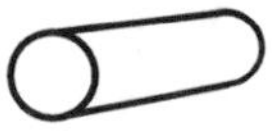 ⬭   d.  ▱

4. How can the figure be described?

   a. equilateral triangle
   b. scalene triangle
   c. isosceles triangle
   d. obtuse triangle

5. Which is not true of similar shapes?

   a. They are the same shape.
   b. They have the same angle measures.
   c. They have different side measures.
   d. They are the same size.

6. Which face can be traced from the solid shown?

   a.  △   b.  ○   c. ☐   d.  ▭

7. Which is not a three-dimensional figure?

   a. sphere   b. cube   c. rectangle d. pyramid

0-7682-2933-2 *Getting Ready to Teach Math for the New Teacher*

•Assessment•
Geometry

8. Name the figure that has 1 square face and 4 triangular faces.

_____

9. A solid figure has 2 round faces and can roll. What is its name? _____

10. The perimeter of the rectangle is 40 inches. What is the length of side R?

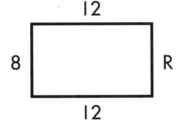

_____

11. What is the area of figure G? Remember to label in square units.

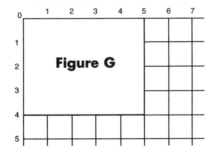

_____

12. How many faces, edges, and vertices make up the rectangular prism shown?

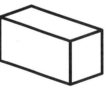

_____ faces   _____ edges   _____ vertices

13. What transformation caused the movement below? _____

14. A 4-sided polygon has 2 parallel sides. The other two sides are not necessarily the same length, and they are not parallel. Name the polygon. _____

0-7682-2933-2 *Getting Ready to Teach Math for the New Teacher*

•Assessment•

Geometry

15. What is the perimeter of the figure? Tell how you know.   10 cm

_____

_____

_____

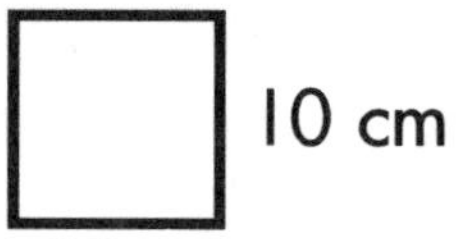

16. Draw a figure similar to the one shown. Draw a figure congruent to the one shown. Explain the difference.

_____

_____

_____

17. Use words and pictures to describe a rhombus. What makes it different from a square?

_____

_____

_____

18. Find the area of the figure. Tell the steps you used.   5 in.

7 in.

_____

_____

_____

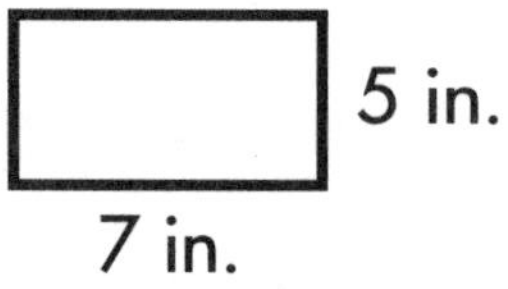

19. Can a rotated figure ever look the same as a reflected figure? Explain. _____

_____

_____

     0-7682-2933-2 *Getting Ready to Teach Math for the New Teacher*

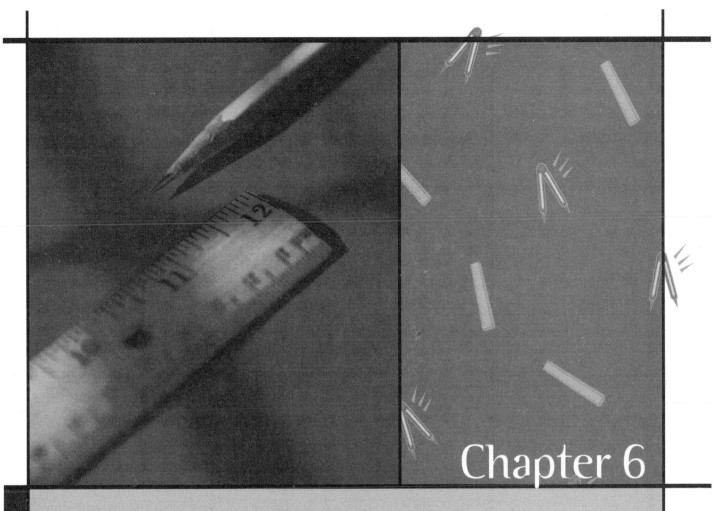

Chapter 6

Measurement Activities

Family Involvement

Invite families to help students learn about measurement. Cooking, weighing groceries, and finding elapsed time between activities are just a few ways that measurement concepts can be reinforced at home.

ELL (English Language Learners)

Invite students from countries where the metric system is used to share their experiences with measurement. American students can benefit from their classmates' knowledge of the metric system. All students can better understand the relationships between measurement systems by sharing experiences.

0-7682-2933-2 *Getting Ready to Teach Math for the New Teacher*

Nearest Inch Measurements

In this activity, students estimate lengths of classroom objects.

1. Distribute an inch ruler to each student. Ask students to identify the inch marks. Then ask volunteers to show where the $\frac{1}{4}$-inch, $\frac{1}{2}$-inch, and $\frac{3}{4}$-inch marks are located.

2. Draw a line $3\frac{3}{4}$ inches long on the board. Ask a student to measure the line with a ruler and tell whether the line is closer to 3 inches or 4 inches in length (4 inches). Repeat the procedure, drawing and having students estimate lengths such as $1\frac{1}{2}$ inches, $2\frac{3}{4}$ inches, and $5\frac{1}{4}$ inches.

3. Draw a line $2\frac{1}{2}$ inches long. Tell students that just as in other estimated amounts, $\frac{1}{2}$-inch measures are estimated up to the next whole inch amount.

4. Have students measure several objects in or around their desks, measuring each to the nearest whole inch. Allow students time to share with each other the objects they measured and compare estimated measurements.

Estimated Metric Lengths

Students create their own images of measurement units in this exploratory activity.

1. Remind students that centimeters and meters are used to measure shorter lengths, while kilometers generally are used to measure longer distances.

2. Distribute metersticks to each group of students. Have students identify a centimeter and a meter on their metersticks.

3. Distribute a base ten unit block to each group of students. Guide them to measure and discover that the block's length on each side is exactly 1 centimeter.

4. Ask students to find three objects in the classroom whose measurements are about 1 centimeter and 1 meter.

5. Allow students time to share their results with the class. Close by asking students to tell how they might determine which tool is best to measure the length of an object. (Students may say that short objects should be measured in centimeters, and longer ones measured in meters.)

Water Ways

Students enjoy learning about customary units of capacity as they complete this activity. If water is unavailable, rice can be substituted.

1. Have students work in small groups. Provide each group with cup, pint, quart, and gallon containers, as well as enough water (or rice) to fill the gallon container.

2. Say, *You have one gallon of water (rice). Your task is to find out how many of the smaller containers equal one gallon. You also must order the containers from least to greatest in capacity.*

3. Allow ample time for exploration. When groups have completed the task, invite them to compare strategies and results. In the event of disagreement, have groups demonstrate their procedures to justify their results.

4. As a class, summarize the activity. Students should find that there are 4 quarts, 8 pints, or 16 cups to a gallon.

5. Extend the activity by having students find the number of pints in a quart, cups in a pint, cups in a quart, and so forth.

Alive Time

In this activity, students calculate how long they have been alive.

1. Distribute a calculator to each student.

2. Have students record their ages in years only. Tell them to use the calculator to multiply their ages by 365—the number of days in a year. You may wish to add two to three additional days for 366-day leap years.

3. Have students find their birthdays on the calendar and count the number of days since their last birthday. This number should be added to the result of Step 2. The sum is the number of days the students have been alive.

4. Ask students how many hours are in a day (24). Ask students how they could find the number of hours they have been alive (multiply by 24). Have students use a calculator to find the number of hours they have been alive.

5. Repeat the procedure for minutes, having students multiply the result of Step 4 by 60.

0-7682-2933-2 *Getting Ready to Teach Math for the New Teacher*

Benchmark Measurements

Students develop their own benchmarks for measuring.

1. Distribute inch rulers to each student.
2. Have students measure and record the following:
   a. The length of the last joint of their thumbs.
   b. The width of their hand from thumb tip to pointer tip.
3. Have students measure objects around the room using their hands. For each measurement, have students record the number of hands or thumb joints and estimate the actual length in inches.
4. Allow time for students to do the actual measurements of the objects using rulers.
5. Engage students in a discussion about their estimates and the actual measures. Emphasize that when they are in need of an approximate measurement in real life, they will always have their hands to help them estimate.

Choose a Unit

Students develop their knowledge of measurement units as they choose the most appropriate unit to measure various classroom objects.

1. Have students create a chart as shown below.

Classroom Object	Measurement Unit	Actual Measure

2. Allow students to complete the chart using ten classroom objects. Students should:
   a. Select the object to measure.
   b. Choose the appropriate measure.
   c. Measure the object.
3. Allow time for students to share their results with classmates.

© McGraw-Hill Children's Publishing

0-7682-2933-2 *Getting Ready to Teach Math for the New Teacher*

Measuring Sports Equipment

Students learn all about a specific piece of sports equipment.

1. Have groups of students choose a favorite sport from the following list: basketball, baseball, football, soccer, golf, or tennis.

2. Each group member chooses one piece of equipment for the sport and measures it in as many ways as possible.

3. Group members combine their findings on a chart. Display charts on the bulletin board.

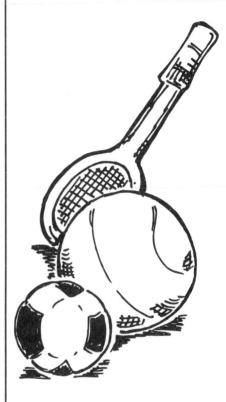

Measurement Conversions

Students reinforce their knowledge of metric measure conversions as they discover multiplication and division patterns.

1. Review the relationship between meters and centimeters. Make certain students recall that there are 100 centimeters in 1 meter.

2. Have students copy and complete the table.

Meters	1	3	5	8	11	20	35
Centimeters	100			800		2,000	

3. Allow time for class discussion about the table. Extend the activity by having students copy and complete tables that focus on other metric relationships, such as the following:

Grams	1,000	4,000	5,000	9,000	10,000	13,000	25,000
Kilograms	1		5		10		

Measure It

Set up a measurement center with scales, thermometer, measuring tape, ruler, measuring cups, etc. Ask each student to bring in something to measure. Have students exchange items, then rotate by groups of four through the measurement center. Ask them to record their data in standard units, then convert it to metric units.

0-7682-2933-2 *Getting Ready to Teach Math for the New Teacher*

Customary Units of Length

Directions: Fill in the blanks with the equivalent measurements.

> 1 foot = 12 inches
> 1 yard = 3 feet
> 1 mile = 5,280 feet

Fill in the blanks with the equivalent measurement.

1. 7 yards = _____ feet

2. 24 inches = _____ feet

3. 6 feet = _____ yard(s)

4. 10 miles = _____ feet

5. 60 inches = _____ feet

6. 30 feet = _____ yard(s)

7. 5 feet + 2 inches = _____ inches

8. 3 feet = _____ inches

9. 1 yard + 4 inches = _____ inches

10. $\frac{1}{2}$ mile = _____ feet

11. 1 yard − 1 foot = _____ feet

12. 46 inches − 10 inches =

_____ yard(s)

13. 4 yards = _____ feet

14. 7 feet − 4 feet = _____ yard(s)

15. 1 yard + 3 inches = _____ inches

0-7682-2933-2 *Getting Ready to Teach Math for the New Teacher*

Name _____ Date _____

Metric Units of Length

Directions: Use the chart. Write the answers.

The metric measuring system is based on multiples of 10.
Below is a chart of metric conversions.

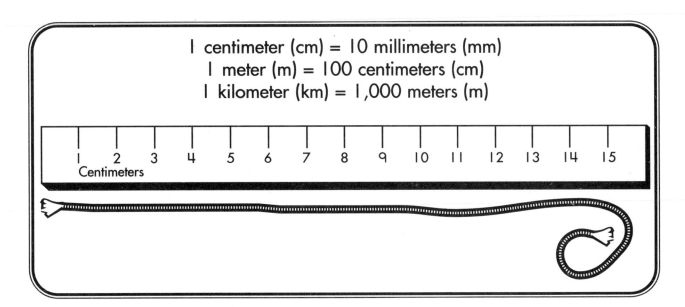

1. Jodi measured her tomato plant.
   It is 34 centimeters. How many millimeters is this? _____

2. Meg has a plastic case that is 4 centimeters long.
   She found a shell that is 34 millimeters long. Will it fit in her case? _____

3. Kifa jumped 3 meters. How many centimeters is this? _____

4. Jordan's desk is 1 meter by 1 meter. He would like to
   put his science project inside his desk. The science
   project is on poster board that is 95 centimeters by
   110 centimeters. Will it fit inside his desk without sticking out? _____

5. Anna is walking in a 5-kilometer charity event. How many
   meters will she walk by the time she reaches the finish line? _____

6. Jonathan is running in the 10,000-meter
   race. How many kilometers is the race? _____

0-7682-2933-2 *Getting Ready to Teach Math for the New Teacher*

Customary Units of Capacity

Directions: Fill in the blanks with the equivalent measurements.

> 1 tablespoon = 3 teaspoons
> 1 cup = 16 tablespoons = 8 fluid ounces
> 1 pint = 2 cups
> 1 quart = 2 pints
> 1 gallon = 4 quarts

1. 18 pints = _____ quarts

2. 28 quarts = _____ pints

3. 10 pints = _____ cups

4. 18 cups = _____ quarts

5. 4 tablespoons = _____ teaspoons

6. 24 quarts = _____ gallons

7. 5 pints = _____ fluid ounces

8. 1 quart = _____ fluid ounces

9. 2 cups = _____ tablespoons

Answer the questions.

10. Jackie drinks one pint of chocolate milk each day with her
    school lunch. How many cups of chocolate milk is that in
    5 days? Does she drink enough in 5 days to fill a gallon? _____

11. Paula has a 20-gallon fish tank. She needs to treat the tank with
    a chemical. The directions say to put one drop in for every quart of
    water. How many drops of chemical are needed for this aquarium? _____

0-7682-2933-2 *Getting Ready to Teach Math for the New Teacher*

Selecting Appropriate Units of Capacity

Directions: Circle the best unit of capacity for measuring the objects and containers below.

Remember!
1000 mL = 1 L
1000 L = 1 kL

1.   mL   L   kL

2.   mL   L   kL

3.   mL   L   kL

4.   mL   L   kL

5.   mL   L   kL

6.   mL   L   kL

7.   mL   L   kL

8.   mL   L   kL

9.   mL   L   kL

10.   mL   L   kL

11.   mL   L   kL

12.   mL   L   kL

113

0-7682-2933-2 *Getting Ready to Teach Math for the New Teacher*

Customary Units of Weight

Directions: Find the following conversions. Show your work.

1. 2 lbs. = _____ oz.

2. 5,000 lbs. = _____ t.

3. 160 oz. = _____ lbs.

4. 6 t. = _____ lbs.

5. 15 lbs. = _____ oz.

6. 20 lbs. = _____ oz.

7. 16,000 lbs. = _____ t.

8. 64 oz. = _____ lbs.

9. 10 lbs. = _____ oz.

> 1 pound (lb.) = 16 ounces (oz.)
> 1 ton (t.) = 2,000 pounds (lbs.)

Answer the questions.

10. Kwaku has a 2-pound bag of soil. How many ounces is the bag? _____

11. A young rhino weighs 2,500 pounds. How many tons is the rhino? _____

12. A particular bridge has a weight capacity of 15 tons.
    A truck's loaded trailer weighs 40,000 pounds.
    Should the trucker drive over the bridge? _____

13. A recipe for apple pie calls for 2 pounds of apples. The
    produce scale says 34 ounces. Are there enough apples for a pie? _____

0-7682-2933-2 *Getting Ready to Teach Math for the New Teacher*

Name _____ Date _____

Selecting Appropriate Units of Mass

Directions: Choose grams (g) or kilograms (kg) to identify the appropriate unit of measurement.

Remember!
1,000 g = 1 kg

1.   g   kg

2.   g   kg

3.   g   kg

4.   g   kg

5.   g   kg

6.   g   kg

7.   g   kg

8.   g   kg

9.   g   kg

10.   g   kg

11.   g   kg

12.   g   kg

0-7682-2933-2 *Getting Ready to Teach Math for the New Teacher*

Brrrr, It's Cold!

Directions: Read each thermometer.
Write the temperature in Fahrenheit and Celsius.

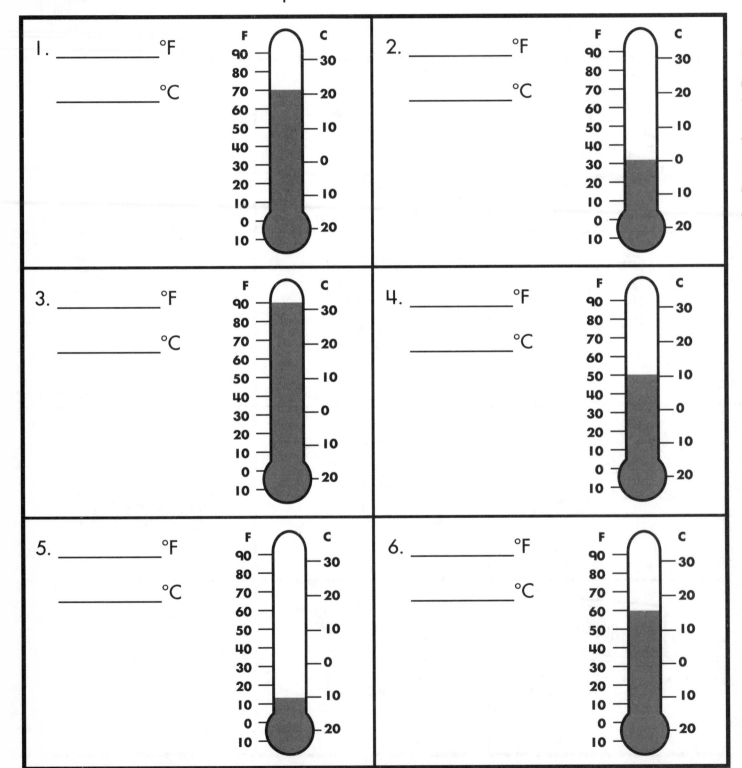

1. _____°F

   _____°C

2. _____°F

   _____°C

3. _____°F

   _____°C

4. _____°F

   _____°C

5. _____°F

   _____°C

6. _____°F

   _____°C

0-7682-2933-2 *Getting Ready to Teach Math for the New Teacher*

A Timely Riddle

Directions: Write the time on the blank under each clock.

C.  _____	E.  _____	F.  _____	H. 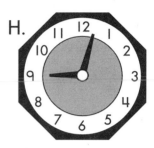 _____
I.  _____	K.  _____	L.  _____	M.  _____
O.  _____	S.  _____	T.  _____	X.  _____

Write the letters from above that go with the times to solve the riddle.
Hint: You will not use every letter, and you may use some more than once.

What time is it when the clock strikes 13?

___ ___ ___ ___   ___ ___   ___ ___ ___
12:12 3:21 4:13 8:42   12:12 6:48   10:23 3:21 9:39

___ ___ ___   ___ ___ ___ ___ ___
12:12 9:02 8:42   11:09 2:34 6:48 11:09 3:58

   0-7682-2933-2 *Getting Ready to Teach Math for the New Teacher*

Measurement

1. A tennis racquet is about 2 ___ long.

    a. miles   b. yards   c. feet   d. inches

2. Which is the best estimate for the capacity of the popcorn container?

    a. 4 ounces   b. 4 cups
    c. 4 quarts   d. 4 gallons

3. Which is the best estimate for the height of a door?

    a. 7 inches b. 7 feet   c. 7 yards d. 7 miles

4. Which is the best measurement tool to find the weight of the puppy?

    a.    b.   c.   d.

5. Which is the best estimate for the weight of the apples?

    a. 30 yds. b. 30 tons
    c. 30 lbs. d. 30 oz.

6. Measure the length of the marker to the nearest inch.

_____

7. Wendy can buy a 2-pound box of pretzels or a bag that weighs 29 ounces. Which weighs more? How much more? _____

_____

8. Randy says he is 4 feet, 3 inches tall. How tall is Randy in inches? _____

    0-7682-2933-2 *Getting Ready to Teach Math for the New Teacher*

Measurement

9. A baseball bat is about one ____ long.

   a. mm   b. cm   c. m   d. km

10. Which is the best estimate for the capacity of the pitcher?

   a. 7 mL   b. 70 mL   c. 700 mL   d. 7 L

11. Which is the best estimate for the mass of the football helmet?

   a. 2 g   b. 20 g   c. 200 g   d. 2 kg

12. Which is the best measurement tool to find the height of the lamp?

   a.   b.

   c.   d.

13. Which is the best measurement tool for the liquid dye?

   a.   b.

   c.    d.

14. Measure the length of the crayon to the nearest centimeter. _____

BLUE

15. Leila bought 3 meters of ribbon. How many centimeters of ribbon did she buy? _____

16. Ben bought a 2-kilogram bag of charcoal. How many grams was it? _____

17. What time is shown on the clock?

   _____

0-7682-2933-2 *Getting Ready to Teach Math for the New Teacher*

•Assessment•
Measurement

18. Mr. Rice jogs from his house to the park several times each day. He says he jogs over 3,000 feet. Is this reasonable? Explain.

_____

_____

_____

19. Yasmine wants to make 4 liters of punch. Her punch bowl holds 3,500 milliliters of liquid. Will the punch fit? Explain.

_____

_____

_____

20. Should Cathy be wearing a heavy jacket or a short-sleeved shirt if the temperature is 29°C? Explain.

_____

_____

_____

21. A baseball coach wants 7 liters of water in a cooler. He only has a 3-liter container and a 5-liter container. How can he measure exactly 7 liters into the cooler?

_____

_____

_____

22. Ms. Woodard's Drama Club starts rehearsal at 9:30 in the morning. They take a half-hour break and practice until 5:00. How long do they rehearse? Tell how you know.

_____

_____

_____

0-7682-2933-2 *Getting Ready to Teach Math for the New Teacher*

Chapter 7

Data Analysis and Probability

Good Advice!

During the unit on graphing, be sure to share actual graphs found in the newspaper with your class. Discuss what makes graphs useful and why they are part of everyday life. Invite students to make or find similar graphs to share with their classmates.

Math Literacy

Help your students become familiar with different types of graphs and their purposes. Students should know that bar graphs are used for comparisons, line graphs show changes and trends over time, and circle graphs compare parts to a whole.

0-7682-2933-2 *Getting Ready to Teach Math for the New Teacher*

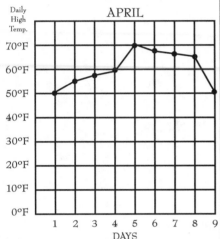

Making a Line Graph

Students practice reading a newspaper weather page as they apply their knowledge of line graphs.

1. Bring the weather page from a daily newspaper to school every day for at least one week.

2. Ask students to create a data table showing the daily high temperatures for the period.

3. Have students use the data and graph paper to plot a line graph.

4. When they finish, have students discuss what the line graph shows. Ask students to talk about the trends in the data. Do the temperatures rise, fall, or remain about the same? What would they predict for the next day's temperature? On what do they base their predictions?

Survey and Analyze

Students conduct surveys and analyze the results.

1. Have students work in small groups. Invite them to decide on a topic for a class. For example, students may decide to collect data about their classmates' favorite playground activity.

2. Ask student groups to decide how they will collect the data and organize it so that it could be shared with the class. Allow time for the actual data collection. Provide supplies needed for students to share the data.

3. Ask each student to write a paragraph describing:
   a. The group's survey;
   b. How the data was collected;
   c. How the data was displayed; and
   d. The information the group learned by analyzing the data.

Students' responses should be clear and complete. They may include sketches or data tables showing the data their groups collected. Analysis should reflect an understanding of the data and how it could be used. Ask students to suggest ways they can interpret the data to form an opinion or make a decision.

Exploring Probability

This simple game enables students to think about the likelihood of events.

1. Have students work in pairs. Provide each pair with a paper bag, six blue cubes, three green cubes, and one yellow cube.

2. Students in each pair take turns predicting which color cube will be picked and then drawing a cube from the bag without looking. If the prediction is correct, the player scores a point. Return the cube to the bag after each turn.

3. Play continues until each child has had 20 turns making predictions. The student with the highest score wins the game.

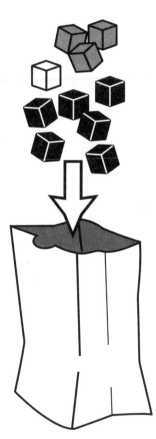

After the game, ask students to write about what happened. Encourage them to describe the probability of drawing a blue, a green, or a yellow cube in terms of *certain, very likely, unlikely,* or *impossible.* Ask them to tell who won the game and why their predictions earned them a winning score. (Students should identify blue as being very likely, green less likely, and yellow unlikely; they should acknowledge that the student who predicted "blue" more often was more likely to win the game, since there were more blue cubes than green or yellow cubes.)

Line Plot Data Collector

In this activity, students integrate their knowledge of line plots and probability.

1. Have students draw a horizontal line on a piece of lined paper. Beneath the line, have them write the numbers 2–12.

2	3	4	5	6	7	8	9	10	11	12

2. Distribute two dice to each group of four students. Have students take turns rolling the dice and stating the resulting sum.

3. Each student records an "X" below the number that tells the sum of the roll. For example, if a student in the group rolls a 4 and a 5, all of the students in the group record an "X" below the 9 on the line plot.

4. Students take turns rolling and recording for a total of 40 rolls.

5. When students have completed the activity, have them discuss their results in groups.

6. Ask students to predict which sum will occur most if it is rolled with two dice. Have students justify their answers using the data on their line plots.

Data Descriptions

Students reinforce what they know about graphs as they complete a writing prompt about them.

1. Ask students to bring graphs from recent newspapers or magazines. Bring in several additional graphs for those students who don't have access to these materials.

2. Review the characteristics of all graphs, including the title, labels, and the information they convey.

3. Have each student write a paragraph describing the data on his graph.

4. Display graphs on one side of a bulletin board and students' descriptive paragraphs on the other side.

5. Have students match the paragraphs with the correct data display.

6. Allow time for students to share their responses and discuss as a class.

Data Descriptions

0-7682-2933-2 *Getting Ready to Teach Math for the New Teacher*

TV Time

Students keep track of their TV-watching habits and use the data.

1. Have students keep track of the time they spend watching TV for a week.

2. Discuss characteristics of a bar graph, including title, labels, and information that correctly reflects the data collected.

3. Have students show their data on the graphs. Students can write two questions and answers based on the bar graph.

4. Ask students to write a paragraph discussing their TV-watching habits. They may include whether they think they watch enough or too much TV, what kinds of shows they prefer, and so forth.

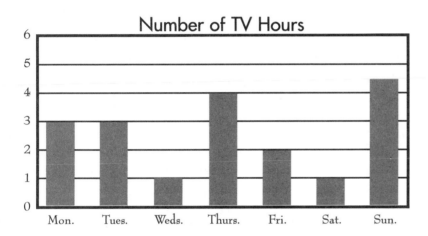

Median and Mode

Students can practice finding the median (the middle number in a data set) and the mode (the number occurring most often in a data set) by using data sets. For each data set, create a master list and display it in a location easily accessible to all students.

- Students' weight in centimeters. (Post a centimeter measuring device near the classroom door. Allow students time to measure themselves or each other.)
- Number of hours per week spent on homework.
- Total number of people or pets living in home.
- Number of minutes spent traveling one way to school.

Math Literacy

Encourage students to use complete sentences and appropriate mathematical terms such as *data*, *graph*, *probable*, *mean*, and *average* when discussing or writing about math. Ongoing practice using correct language enhances students' understanding of mathematical concepts.

125

Mean

Students will construct their own algorithmic procedure for finding the mean average.

1. Arrange students in small groups. Distribute between 5 and 20 two-color counters or cubes to each student, making sure that no two students in a group have the same number of counters.

2. Challenge students to redistribute their counters so they each have the same amount, with leftover counters placed in the center of the workspace.

3. Ask students to report their procedures. Guide students to say that they collected all the counters in one large group, then distributed them evenly amongst themselves.

4. Use one group's example to model the algorithmic procedure on the board. Write the numbers of counters given: 2, 11, 8, and 17. When they put them together, they added. Find the sum (38). When they redistributed evenly, they divided. Divide 38 by 4, since there were four students. The quotient is 9, with 2 remaining. Confirm that each student has nine counters with two left over.

5. Have students complete the algorithmic procedure using their own numbers to check their manipulative work.

The Language of Math

In the classroom, it is important for students to hear the language of mathematics in meaningful contexts. Enrich your math program with classroom activities that introduce and reinforce mathematics as a simple language that students easily can understand and use.

© McGraw-Hill Children's Publishing   0-7682-2933-2 *Getting Ready to Teach Math for the New Teacher*

Name _____ Date _____

What's in a Name?

Directions: The pictograph shows the number of letters in students' first names. Use the pictograph to answer the questions.

Letters in Our First Names

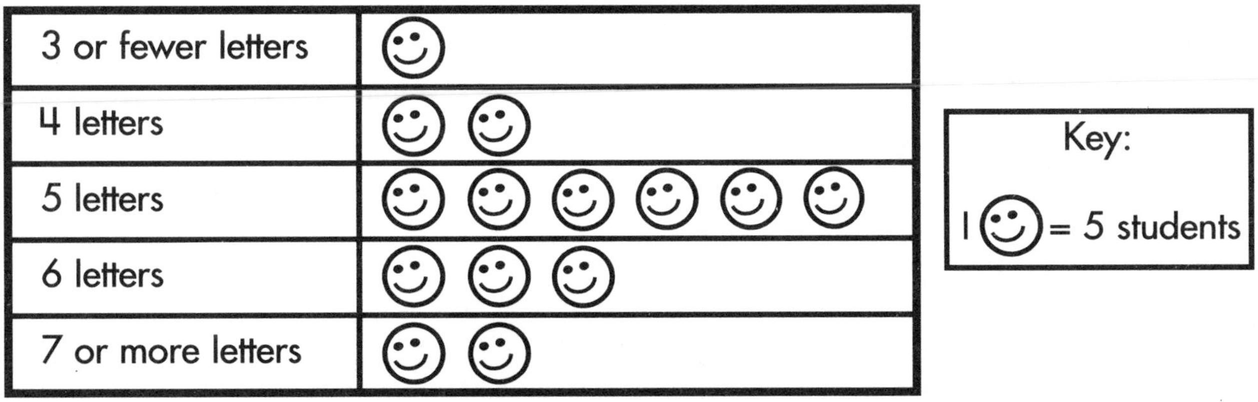

3 or fewer letters	☺
4 letters	☺ ☺
5 letters	☺ ☺ ☺ ☺ ☺ ☺
6 letters	☺ ☺ ☺
7 or more letters	☺ ☺

Key:
1 ☺ = 5 students

1. What does each symbol stand for? _____

2. How many students' first names contain 6 letters? _____

3. How many students' first names contain 4 letters? _____

4. How many letters long are 30 students' names? _____

5. How many students are shown on this pictograph? _____

6. How many more students have names with 4 letters than with 3 or fewer letters? _____

7. Suppose 25 more students say they have 3 or fewer letters in their names. How would the pictograph change? _____

_____

_____

8. Write a question about the graph. Then answer the question. _____

_____

_____

127

0-7682-2933-2 *Getting Ready to Teach Math for the New Teacher*

Name _____ Date _____

Be a Sport

Directions: The bar graph shows favorite sports of third-grade students. Use the bar graph to answer the questions.

Our Favorite Sports

Baseball		
Football		
Karate		
Soccer		
Swimming		

0 2 4 6 8 10 12 14

1. Which sport was chosen by 8 students? _____

2. Which sport was chosen by 4 students? _____

3. How many more students chose karate than swimming? _____

4. Which two sports were chosen by the same number of students? _____

5. Which sport was chosen by the greatest number of students? _____

   How many students chose it? _____

6. How many more students would need to choose football in order for it to have the same number of votes as soccer? _____

7. Write a question about the graph. Then answer the question. _____

   _____

   _____

0-7682-2933-2 *Getting Ready to Teach Math for the New Teacher*

Line Plots

Directions: A line plot is a graph that shows data by using symbols that are lined up. This line plot shows how many visits each of the students in the science club made to the school media center in one month.

Use the line plot to answer the questions.

School Media Center Visits

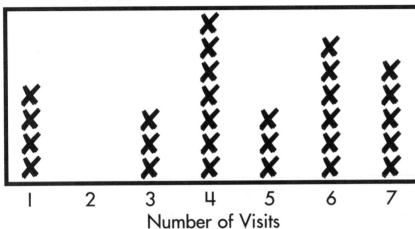

1. What was the most common number of visits made by students this month? _____

2. How many students visited the Media Center 6 times during the month? _____

3. In all, how many students visited the Media Center 3, 4, or 5 times during the month? _____

4. How many students' responses are shown on the line plot? _____

5. Are there any gaps in the line plot? _____

   If so, what does it mean? _____

6. Write a fraction to show how many students visited the Media Center 4 times in the month. (Write it in lowest terms.)_____

7. How many times did 25% of the students visit the Media Center during the month? _____

8. Write a question about the graph for a classmate to answer. _____

   _____

0-7682-2933-2 *Getting Ready to Teach Math for the New Teacher*

Line Graphs

Directions: A line graph shows data that changes over time. This line graph shows the number of miles Marci ran each week during an eight-week period.

Use the line graph to answer the questions.

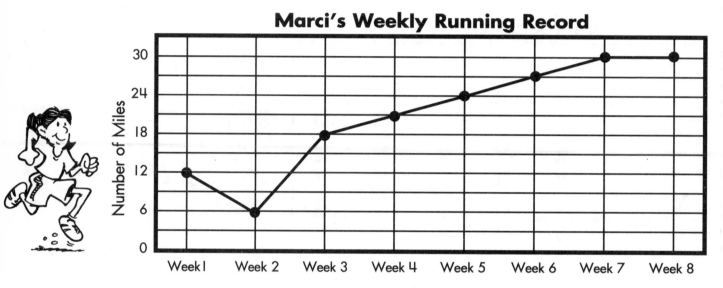

Marci's Weekly Running Record

1. How many miles did Marci run during week 2? _____

2. How many miles did Marci run during week 5? _____

3. During which week did the number of miles decrease? _____

4. During which week did the number of miles increase the most? _____

5. How many miles did Marci run in all during the eight weeks? _____

6. How many more miles did Marci run during week 5 than during week 2? _____

7. What was the average number of miles Marci ran per week? _____

8. Predict the number of miles Marci will run in week 9. Give an explanation for your answer. _____

_____

9. Write a question about the graph for a classmate to answer. _____

_____

0-7682-2933-2 *Getting Ready to Teach Math for the New Teacher*

Median, Mode, and Range

Directions: For each of the following number groups, list the median, mode, and range. **Hint:** For some, you will need to rearrange the numbers in numerical order first.

The **median** is the number that is in the middle when a group of numbers is arranged in order from least to greatest.

The **mode** is the number that occurs most often.

To find the **range**, subtract the least number from the greatest.

Example:

20 25 26 26 26 26 32 33 34 34 35 37 39

The **median** is 32.

The **mode** is 26.

The **range** is 19.

---

1. 13 14 14 14 15 17 17 19 21

   median _____   mode _____

   range _____

2. 50 52 52 52 53 56 57 58 60

   median _____   mode _____

   range _____

3. 6 9 10 12 14 14 15

   median _____   mode _____

   range _____

4. 82 86 91 80 82 82 89

   median _____   mode _____

   range _____

5. 71 73 73 73 74 76 79

   median _____   mode _____

   range _____

6. 5 4 4 8 3 2 1

   median _____   mode _____

   range _____

7. 31 32 33 34 35 36 36

   median _____   mode _____

   range _____

8. 10 32 27 25 37 16 25

   median _____   mode _____

   range _____

0-7682-2933-2 *Getting Ready to Teach Math for the New Teacher*

Take a Chance

1.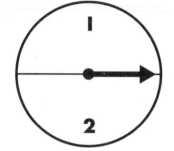

1: __1__ out of __2__

2: __1__ out of __2__

2.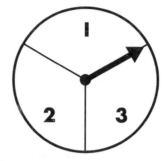

1: ___ out of ___

2: ___ out of ___

3.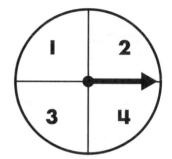

1: ___ out of ___

2: ___ out of ___

4.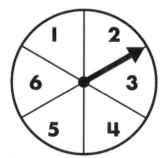

1: ___ out of ___

2: ___ out of ___

5.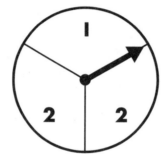

1: ___ out of ___

2: ___ out of ___

6.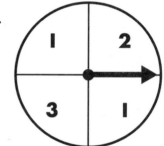

1: ___ out of ___

2: ___ out of ___

7.

1: ___ out of ___

2: ___ out of ___

8.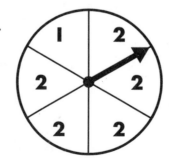

1: ___ out of ___

2: ___ out of ___

9.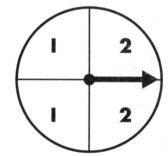

1: ___ out of ___

2: ___ out of ___

0-7682-2933-2 *Getting Ready to Teach Math for the New Teacher*

Data Analysis and Probability

Use the graph to answer questions 1.–5.

Travel Time to School

5 Minutes	👤👤👤👤
10 Minutes	👤👤👤👤👤👤
15 Minutes	👤👤👤👤👤👤👤👤
20 Minutes	👤👤👤👤
25 Minutes	👤👤

👤 = 1 student

1. How many students need about 10 minutes to get to school?

   a. 4 students   b. 6 students
   c. 10 students   d. 26 students

2. How many students need 15 minutes or longer to get to school?

   a. 7 students   b. 14 students
   c. 16 students   d. 26 students

3. How many students' responses are shown on the pictograph?

   a. 7 students   b. 16 students
   c. 22 students   d. 26 students

4. What is the most popular travel time to school?_____

5. If you added your travel time to the graph, how would the graph change?

   _____

   _____

A bag of candy contains the following:

Red: 7   Blue: 6   Green: 5   Purple: 2   Yellow: 6   Brown: 7   Orange: 7

6. What is the mode for the data?

   a. 7   b. 6   c. 5   d. 4

7. What is the median of the data?

   a. 7   b. 6   c. 5   d. 4

8. Explain the difference between the median and the mode? _____

_____

© McGraw-Hill Children's Publishing   0-7682-2933-2 *Getting Ready to Teach Math for the New Teacher*

Data Analysis and Probability

Use the bar graph to
answer questions 9.–13.

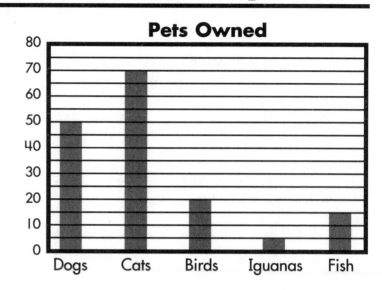

Pets Owned

9. How many more people
   own cats than dogs?

   a. 5 people   b. 10 people
   c. 15 people   d. 20 people

10. How many pets are
    represented by the survey?

    a. 155 pets   b. 160 pets
    c. 175 pets   d. 200 pets

11. How many dogs and cats are there in all? _____

12. How many fewer people own iguanas than fish? _____

13. How many more fish would be needed to make the
    same number of fish and birds? Tell how you know. _____

_____

Use the line plot to
answer questions 14.–16.

14. What is the most popular number
    of visits made by students this month?

    a. 3 visits   b. 4 visits
    c. 6 visits   d. 7 visits

School Media Center Visits

15. How many students visited the media center 6 times during the month?

    a. 4 students   b. 5 students   c. 6 students   d. 7 students

16. Why does "2 visits" have no X's on the line plot? _____

          0-7682-2933-2 *Getting Ready to Teach Math for the New Teacher*

Name _____ Date _____

Data Analysis and Probability

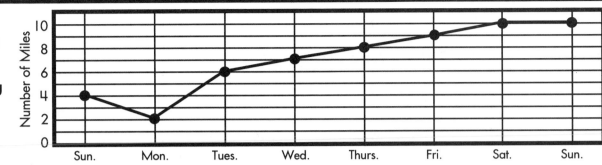

Marci's Daily Running Record

Use the line graph to answer questions 17.–23.

17. How many miles did Marci run on Monday?

    a. 4 miles   b. 3 miles   c. 2 miles   d. 1 mile

18. Between which two days did the number of miles decrease?

    a. between Sunday and Monday   b. between Monday and Tuesday
    c. between Thursday and Friday   d. between Saturday and Sunday

19. Between which two days did the number of miles increase the most?

    a. between Sunday and Monday   b. between Monday and Tuesday
    c. between Thursday and Friday   d. between Saturday and Sunday

20. How many miles did Marci run on Saturday and Sunday combined?
Write a number sentence to show how you found your answer. _____

_____

21. How many more miles did Marci run on Thursday than on Wednesday?
Write a number sentence to show how you found your answer. _____

_____

22. Make a prediction about the number of miles Marci will run on the Monday
after the second Sunday (it is not shown on the graph). Justify your answer._____

_____

23. Write a question that can be answered using the line graph.
Then answer your question. _____

_____

      0-7682-2933-2 *Getting Ready to Teach Math for the New Teacher*

Data Analysis and Probability

Use the data to answer questions 24.–28.

Raul's test scores are: 79, 92, 78, 100, 96, 86, 97, 100.

24. What is the mode of the test scores? _____

25. What is the median of the test scores? _____

26. What is the mean of the test scores? _____

27. Describe how you found the mean. _____

_____

28. Raul can ask his teacher to use the mean, median, or mode for his final
    grade. Which should he ask his teacher to use? Explain your answer. _____

_____

_____

29. A counter will be picked from the bag without
    looking. What is the likelihood that it will be black?

    a. certain   b. likely
    c. not likely   d. impossible

30. A number is drawn from a facedown deck of number cards.
    What is the likelihood that a 10 will be drawn?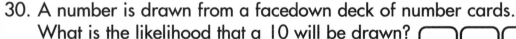

    a. certain   b. likely
    c. not likely   d. impossible

31. What is the probability
    that a 2 will be spun?
    Explain your thinking.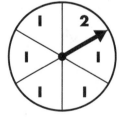

_____

_____

Hundred Chart

1	2	3	4	5	6	7	8	9	10
11	12	13	14	15	16	17	18	19	20
21	22	23	24	25	26	27	28	29	30
31	32	33	34	35	36	37	38	39	40
41	42	43	44	45	46	47	48	49	50
51	52	53	54	55	56	57	58	59	60
61	62	63	64	65	66	67	68	69	70
71	72	73	74	75	76	77	78	79	80
81	82	83	84	85	86	87	88	89	90
91	92	93	94	95	96	97	98	99	100

0-7682-2933-2 *Getting Ready to Teach Math for the New Teacher*

Centimeter Grid Paper

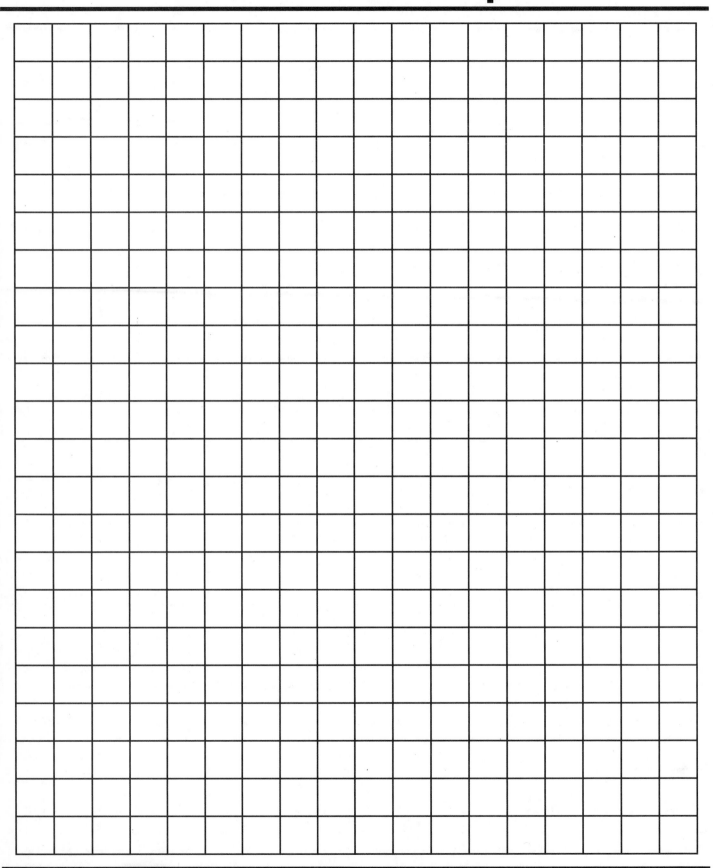

0-7682-2933-2 *Getting Ready to Teach Math for the New Teacher*

Tangram

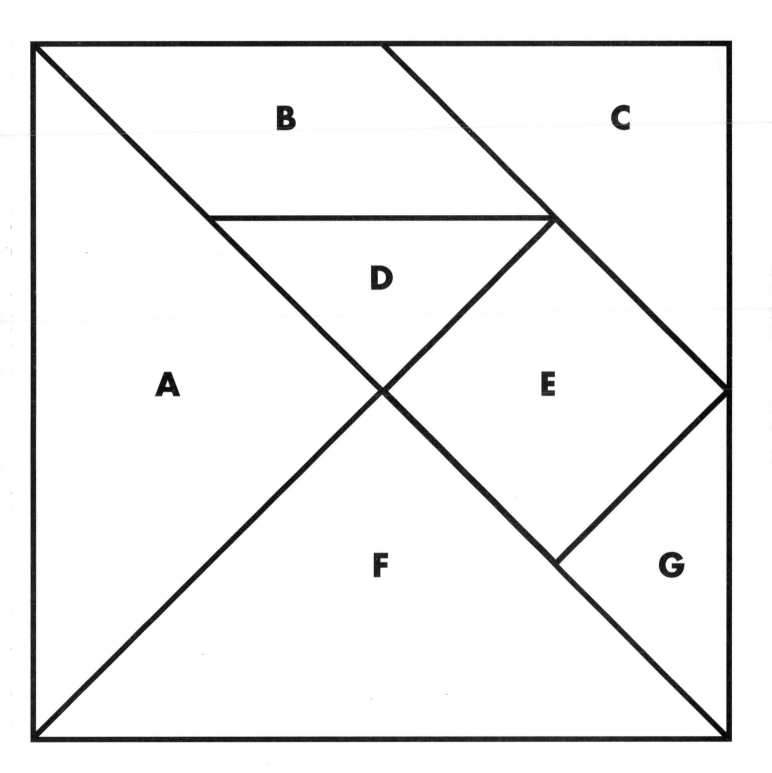

0-7682-2933-2 *Getting Ready to Teach Math for the New Teacher*

Cross-Number Puzzle, Page 29

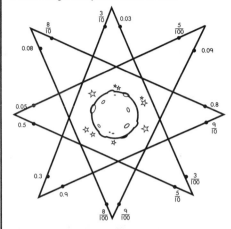

A3	4	B9	8			C1	D2	6	E7
5		3					0		1
0		F1	G3	5		H4	I5	6	
J8	2	4	1		K8	9	4		
		L2	M5	2			N3	O2	
P4	Q2	3	7		R3	0	5		
S9	0	3		3		9			
9			4		1	0			

I'd Walk a Mile, Page 30

1. 743; O
2. 998; N
3. 897; E
4. 231; T
5. 802; H
6. 991; U
7. 7,165; S
8. 5,032; A
9. 7,914; D
10. 6,875; S
11. 8,795; V
12. 5,794; R
13. 4,190; I
14. 9,100; X
15. 7,910; Y

ONE THOUSAND SEVEN HUNDRED SIXTY

Pull Apart, Page 31

1. 4   a. $\frac{1}{4}$ b. $\frac{1}{4}$ c. $\frac{2}{4} = \frac{1}{2}$
   d. $\frac{3}{4}$ e. $\frac{4}{4} = 1$

2. 3   a. $\frac{1}{3}$ b. $\frac{1}{3}$ c. $\frac{1}{3}$
   d. $\frac{2}{3}$ e. $\frac{2}{3}$

3. 7   a. $\frac{2}{7}$ b. $\frac{1}{7}$ c. $\frac{3}{7}$
   d. $\frac{1}{7}$ e. $\frac{4}{7}$ f. $\frac{3}{7}$

4. 5   a. $\frac{1}{5}$ b. $\frac{2}{5}$ c. $\frac{2}{5}$
   d. $\frac{3}{5}$ e. $\frac{4}{5}$ f. $\frac{5}{5} = 1$

Fraction Lineup, Page 32

1. $\frac{1}{2}$; T   2. $\frac{3}{4}$; H   3. $\frac{1}{2}$; E
4. $\frac{3}{5}$; Y   5. $\frac{3}{8}$; N   6. $\frac{3}{4}$; V
7. $\frac{2}{3}$; R   8. $\frac{7}{8}$; S   9. $\frac{2}{3}$; O
10. THEY NEVER SEE EYE TO EYE.

Match Made in Heaven, Page 33
What design did you make? A star.

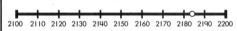

Leaping Along, Page 34

1. 3.7 > 3.4   2.5 < 2.9   4.2 < 5.2
2. 6.1 < 6.8   4.6 > 3.6   8.9 < 9.5
3. 2.8 < 3.1   1.7 > 1.1   4.3 > 4.0
4. 3.5 < 3.6   9.8 > 8.9   7.3 > 6.8
5. 3.1 < 3.8   1.4 < 2.6   3.5 < 3.9
6. 4.8 < 5.1   6.2 < 6.5   5.7 < 5.8
7. 6.3 > 5.8   7.2 < 7.3   8.5 < 9.2
8. 2.0, 2.3, 2.4   9. 6.2, 6.5, 6.7
10. 4.9, 5.0, 5.1
11. Answers will vary.

School Store Shopping, Page 35

1. $0.75 change   2. $0.61 change
3. $0.45 change   4. $0.33 change
5. $0.27 change   6. Yes
7. Yes

Assessment—Whole Numbers, Pages 36–37

1. b   2. c   3. b   4. d
5. d   6. 721,085
7. 1,001; 1,010; 1,011, 1,100
8. 788,987 < 789,101
9. a. 8,000   b. 8,400
10. a. 4,215
    b. 4000 + 200 + 10 + 5
11. Answers will vary but must include: 1,999; 2,000; 2,001; 2,002; 2,003; and 2,004.
12. Order the thousands first. Since 7,000 is less than 8,000; 7,970 is the smallest number. Order by hundreds. There are 0 hundreds in all three numbers, so order by tens. 8,036 is next because 3 tens is less than 9 tens. Order

by ones. 2 is less than 5, so 8,092 is less than 8,095. In order from least to greatest, the numbers are 7,970; 8,036; 8,092; and 8,095.
13. Bonita came in second, because after 5,003, 4,808 is the next highest number.
14. Sherry rounds the number 762. She uses the digits 2, 6, and 7 so that there are 7 hundreds; and the number of tens is greater than 5 so it can be rounded to the next higher hundred.
15. Answers may vary.

To round 2,184 to the nearest hundred, plot it on a number line between 2,100 and 2,200. Since 2,184 is closer to 2,200 than to 2,100, it rounds to 2,200.

Assessment—Fractions and Decimals, Pages 38–40

1. d   2. a   3. c
4.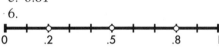
5. 0.67
6.

7. $\frac{3}{7} > \frac{2}{7}$

8. Students' pictures should show a region with 6 sections, 5 of which are colored.
9. Students' pictures should show 10 items, 7 of which are shaded.
10. Bill is incorrect. $\frac{1}{4}$ is less than $\frac{1}{3}$. In order to make a whole out of fourths, 4 pieces are needed. For the same whole made of thirds, only 3 pieces are needed.
11. Two and five hundredths; two and five tenths. Two and five tenths is greater because it is two wholes and five out of ten sections. Two and five hundredths has the same two wholes, but has only 5 out of 100 sections.
12. 0.5 or 0.50. Five tenths and fifty hundredths are equivalent to $\frac{1}{2}$; the numerator is half of the denominator.
13. $1.55. Students may draw a nickel, 2 quarters, and a dollar bill; counting up from $3.45 to $5.00 with each coin or bill.

0-7682-2933-2 *Getting Ready to Teach Math for the New Teacher*

Color by Sum, Page 50

Flower petals labeled: purple, purple, yellow, red, red, purple, purple, purple, yellow, red, orange, red, yellow, red, orange, orange, orange

Describe the number patterns that you see.
Each flower has the same sum in the center
and the same sum for all the petals.

Nines Are Fine, Page 51

836 + 90 = 926	536 + 248 = 784	952 + 8 = 960	362 + 47 = 409	486 + 293 = 779
789 526 214 = 1,529	2,846 + 6,478 = 9,324	932 + 365 = 1,297	374 + 299 = 673	956 874 65 = 1,895
4,768 + 2,894 = 7,662	38 456 3,894 = 4,388	4,507 + 2,743 = 7,250	404 + 289 = 693	1,843 + 6,752 = 8,595
639 77 679 = 1,608	587 342 1,865 2,348 = 4,542	5,379 1,865 2,348 = 4,542	450 + 145 = 595	594 + 278 = 872
29 875 2,341 = 3,245	387 29 5,614 = 6,030	462 379 248 = 1,089		

M-A-T-H-O, Page 52

1. 644, 233, 245, 367, 260
2. 346, 192, 718, 104, 547
3. 304, 703, 382, 452, 85
4. 450, 789, 371, 801, 598

M	A	T	H	O
450	192	382	200	85
644	789	598	452	346
703	718	400	245	304
600	371	233	547	300
104	500	260	367	801

A Greenhouse, Page 53

1. 5,585 impatiens
2. 1,092 long-stem roses
3. 467 four-inch-pot geraniums
4. 1,360 orchids   5. 2,163 tulips
6. 1,233 daisies   7. 3,995 flowers

Catalog Shopping, Page 54

1. $0.62   2. $2.18   3. $4.10
4. $7.59   5. $2.44   6. $4.06
7. Answers will vary.

Match Game, Page 55

1. 10; T   2. 20; U   3. 30; R
4. 45; N   5. 80; A   6. 18; R
7. 40; O   8. 16; U   9. 14; N
10. 70; D   11. 12; F   12. 35; A
13. 60; C   14. 25; T   15. 100; S
16. These pairs of multiplication sentences
    are called TURNAROUND FACTS.

Division Touchdowns, Page 56

1. 21 ÷ 7 = 3   2. 24 ÷ 3 = 8
3. 27 ÷ 9 = 3   4. 48 ÷ 8 = 6
5. 18 ÷ 9 = 2   6. 45 ÷ 5 = 9
7. 42 ÷ 7 = 6   8. 56 ÷ 8 = 7
9. 49 ÷ 7 = 7   10. 63 ÷ 7 = 9
11. 36 ÷ 6 = 6   12. 40 ÷ 8 = 5

True or False?, Page 57

1. T: 7 x 3 = 21; F: 8 x 5 ≠ 41 (40);
   T: 9 x 3 = 27
2. T: 7 x 0 = 0; F: 9 x 7 ≠ 67 (63);
   F: 7 x 7 ≠ 51 (49)
3. F: 9 x 2 ≠ 19 (18); T: 7 x 2 = 14;
   F: 8 x 2 ≠ 17 (16)
4. T: 8 x 9 = 72; F: 7 x 4 ≠ 29 (28);
   T: 8 x 0 = 0
5. F: 9 x 6 ≠ 53 (54); T: 8 x 10 = 80;
   F: 7 x 5 ≠ 37 (35)
6. F: 7 x 6 ≠ 43 (42); F: 9 x 8 ≠ 73 (72);
   T: 9 x 5 = 45
7. F: 7 x 7 = 47 (49); F: 8 x 7 ≠ 57 (56);
   F: 8 x 4 ≠ 33 (32)
8. F: 9 x 0 ≠ 9 (0); F: 9 x 9 ≠ 83 (81);
   F: 9 x 10 ≠ 19 (90)
9. T: 8 x 8 = 64; T: 9 x 4 = 36;
   F: 8 x 3 ≠ 23 (24)
10. T: 7 x 8 = 56; F: 8 x 6 ≠ 47 (48);
    F: 7 x 9 = 69 (63)
True statements < false statements

Multiplication Wizard, Page 58

1. 702; 1,116; 372
2. 927; 996; 754; 2,184; 832
3. 1,146; 834; 504; 714; 790
4. 618; 972; 672; 885; 384
5. 540; 875; 618; 872; 816
6. 784; 638; 768; 660; 762
7. Answers will vary.

The Amusement Park, Page 59

1. 2,303 workers   2. 615 feet
3. 200 times   4. 1,206 children
5. 2,590 people   6. 762 feet high
7. 6,328 people

Diamonds Are Forever, Page 60

A. 28   B. 21   D. 79
E. 31 R3   F. 30   I. 48 R3
L. 43   N. 21 R3   O. 41 R1
S. 44 R3   T. 41   U. 41 R3
ON A BASEBALL FIELD

Division Check Mates, Page 61

1. 18   2. 21
3. 92   4. 42
5. 59   6. 63
7. 82   8. 100
9. 78   10. 39

Think About Remainders, Page 62

1. 3 pairs of socks   2. 47 groups
3. 46 boxes   4. 41 loaves
5. 10 pages   6. 3 tapes
7. 13 vans   8. 34 bottles
9. Answers will vary.

Sports Center, Page 63

1. 6 hooks   2. $19.16
3. 84 golf balls
4. 27 cans of tennis balls
5. 55 T-shirts   6. 108 swim goggles
7. 351 racquetballs
8. 49 mitts   9. Answers will vary

Shady Sums, Page 64

1. $\frac{3}{5}$ 2. $\frac{2}{3}$ 3. $\frac{8}{10}$ 4. $\frac{7}{8}$

5. $\frac{5}{12}$ 6. $\frac{7}{7}$ 7. $\frac{5}{7}$ 8. $\frac{9}{11}$

9. $\frac{4}{5}$ 10. $\frac{9}{12}$ 11. $\frac{4}{6}$ 12. $\frac{7}{10}$

13. $\frac{3}{8}$ 14. $\frac{11}{12}$

What's the Difference?, Page 65

1. $\frac{1}{9}$ 2. $\frac{2}{3}$ 3. $\frac{7}{10}$ 4. $\frac{1}{12}$

5. $\frac{2}{7}$ 6. $\frac{1}{4}$ 7. $\frac{4}{8}$ 8. $\frac{3}{5}$

9. $\frac{1}{12}$ 10. $\frac{3}{7}$ 11. $\frac{4}{7}$ 12. $\frac{2}{11}$

13. $\frac{2}{8}$ 14. $\frac{1}{6}$ 15. $\frac{5}{10}$ 16. $\frac{4}{8}$

0-7682-2933-2 *Getting Ready to Teach Math for the New Teacher*

Word to the Wise, Page 66

3.6 + 1.9 5.5	8.7 − 4.2 4.5	6.5 − 0.9 5.6	2.45 + 3.04 5.49	8.9 − 2.4 6.5
1.25 + 4.40 5.65	7.3 − 2.0 5.3	2.79 + 3.00 5.79	0.6 + 4.4 5.0	4.2 + 1.3 5.5
1.98 + 3.53 5.51	7.86 − 2.30 5.56	4.98 + 0.60 5.58	3.52 + 1.97 5.49	9.9 − 4.4 5.5
5.2 + 0.9 6.1	8.96 − 3.81 5.15	4.9 + 1.9 6.8	2.5 + 2.7 5.2	7.3 − 1.7 5.6
4.55 + 1.00 5.55	6.8 − 1.4 5.4	7.75 − 2.25 5.50	9.31 − 4.00 5.31	3.5 + 2.1 5.6

What word do you see? Hi.

Assessment—Whole Number Addition and Subtraction, Pages 67–68

1. c 2. b 3. d 4. d
5. d 6. b 7. 2,897
8. 141 9. $2.92
10. About 300 more students at McLean
11. 3,038.
Add to check: 3,038 + 964 = 4,002.
12. The sum of 5,612 + 1,920 is greater than the sum of 5,612 + 1,290. One of the addends, 5,612, is the same. The other addend is different. The greater addend produces the greater sum.
5,612 + 1,920 = 7,532.
5,612 + 1,290 = 6,902.
7,532 > 6,902.
13. To estimate the difference, round 771 and 386 to the nearest hundred. 771 rounds to 800. 386 rounds to 400. 800–400 is 400, so about 400 bushes are sold during the season.
14. Number pairs and explanations will vary, but students may say that they found one number pair by subtracting a number (addend) from 5,656 and using the answer as the other addend. Subtracting an amount from one addend and adding to the other may make additional number pairs.
15. Students' answers will vary. Make sure that the total cost is less than 1,200 and the explanation matches the work.

Assessment—Multiplication and Division Facts, Pages 69–71

1. d 2. c 3. b 4. b
5. d 6. 8 x 7 = 56 7. 18
8. 3 x 6; 9 x 2; 2 x 9.
All have a product of 18.
9. 15 tomato plants 10. d
11. c 12. a 13. b 14. c
15. 35 ÷ 7 = 5; 35 ÷ 5 = 7 16. 7
17. Answers will vary, but should have a quotient of 8.
18. 9 pages
19. Students' arrays should have 6 rows with 7 objects, or 7 rows with 6 objects. The product is 42. Explanations will vary.
20. Students' number lines should show three 6-unit jumps. The product is 18. Students' explanations should include a range from 0 to 18 with 3 jumps, each the same distance (6 units).
21. a. If Germaine trades nickels for pennies, he will get 60 pennies because each nickel is worth 5 pennies and 12 x 5 = 60.
b. If Germaine trades his nickels for dimes, he will get 6 dimes because two nickels are needed for each dime and 12 ÷ 2 = 6.
22. Check students' pictures. Facts should include 7 x 8 = 56; 8 x 7 = 56; 56 ÷ 7 = 8; 56 ÷ 8 = 7.

Assessment—Whole Number Multiplication and Division, Pages 72–73

1. a 2. d 3. c 4. b
5. d 6. c 7. 1,256
8. 122 R2 9. $182 10. 26
11. Students' pictures will vary, but should show 3 groups of 32. The product is 96.
12. Descriptions will vary, but students should describe trying to divide 2 hundreds by 5 but not being able to; dividing 21 tens by 5 and having 4 tens in each group, regrouping the remaining 1 ten as 10 ones; and dividing 15 ones by 5 for 3 in each group. The quotient is 43.
13. The greater quotient comes from dividing 487 by 6, since 6 is a smaller divisor. When the dividend is the same, the smaller the divisor is, the greater the quotient will be. To check, 487 ÷ 6 = 81 R1 and 487 ÷ 9 = 54 R1. 81 R1 > 54 R1, so the explanation makes sense.
14. 77 R2. To check, multiply 77 by 8. The product is 616. Add the remaining 2; 616 + 2 = 618.
15. The product must be less than $700, because 7 x $100 is $700, and $76.65 is less than $100.
16. There are 32 slices of pizza. If each person eats 2 pieces, there are 16 people eating pizza. Ahmed ate 2 pieces, so he invited 15 friends.

Assessment—Fractions and Decimals, Page 74

1. c 2. b 3. d
4. d 5. 1.3 kg 6. $\frac{2}{3}$ cups
7. The sum is $\frac{12}{12}$, or 1. The answers are equivalent because $\frac{12}{12}$ is the same as 12 out of 12 pieces, which is equal to one whole.
8. Subtract to solve because the two lengths need to be compared. Align the decimals by the decimal points and subtract. The difference is 2.8 yards. To check, add 2.8 + 2.35. The sum is 5.15.
9. The difference is 0.5 or $\frac{5}{10}$.

Pattern Match, Page 80

1. 7, 9; +2 2. 60, 40, 30; –10
3. 29, 36, 43; +7
4. 27, 24, 21, 18; –3
5. 70, 55, 40, 25; –15
6. 37, 28, 19, 10 –9
7. 41, 49, 57, 65; +8
8. 90, 72, 66, 60; –6
9. 77, 55, 33, 22; –11
10. 48, 60, 72, 84; +12

Nifty Number Patterns, Page 81

1	2	3	4	5	6	7	8	9	10
2	4	6	8	10	12	14	16	18	20
3	6	9	12	15	18	21	24	27	30
4	8	12	16	20	24	28	32	36	40
5	10	15	20	25	30	35	40	45	50
6	12	18	24	30	36	42	48	54	60
7	14	21	28	35	42	49	56	63	70
8	16	24	32	40	48	56	64	72	80
9	18	27	36	45	54	63	72	81	90
10	20	30	40	50	60	70	80	90	100

25 squares have circles. Seven squares have both a circle and an X.

Input-Output, Page 82

1. 16, 12, 10, 6, 18, 4, 14, 2, 8, 0
2. 20, 8, 28, 36, 0, 24, 4, 12, 32, 16
3. 42, 63, 7, 56, 21, 35, 0, 14, 28, 49
4. 20, 10, 40, 15, 35, 45, 0, 30, 5, 25

5. 21, 9, 18, 27, 6, 0, 24, 15, 3, 12
6. 54, 18, 30, 12, 48, 36, 0, 42, 24, 6
7. 24, 64, 32, 72, 0, 8, 56, 40, 16, 48
8. 18, 72, 9, 36, 63, 27, 81, 54, 0, 45

Division Rules! Page 83
1. Rule: Divide by 5
   Out: 1, 2, 3, 4, 5, 6, 7, 8, 9, 10
2. Rule: Divide by 2
   Out: 10, 9, 8, 7, 6, 5, 4, 3, 2, 1
3. Rule: Divide by 3
   Out: 6, 5, 7, 3, 1, 10, 2, 4, 8, 9
4. Rule: Divide by 9
   Out: 10, 1, 9, 2, 8, 3, 7, 4, 6, 5
5. Rule: Divide by 4
   Out: 5, 10, 3, 8, 1, 6, 4, 9, 2, 7
6. Rule: Divide by 8
   Out: 10, 5, 9, 4, 8, 3, 7, 2, 6, 1

Missing Numbers, Page 84
Puzzle One: 48, 8, 4, 36, 6, 18, 2, 7, 28, 14
Puzzle Two: 9, 9, 8, 4, 24, 3, 5, 7, 8, 8
Puzzle Three: 5, 9, 6, 12, 3, 7, 4, 20, 10, 30

Number Letters, Page 85
1. $m = 26$ 2. $a = 16$ 3. $s = 58$
4. $t = 38$ 5. $u = 31$ 6. $o = 19$
7. $b = 20$ 8. $f = 73$ 9. $e = 40$
10. $d = 52$ 11. $r = 23$ 12. $l = 22$
13. $n = 42$ 14. $g = 18$ 15. $c = 17$
Message: Number letters don't scare me.

Assessment—Algebra, Pages 86–88
1. c   2. d   3. c   4. d
5. First 10 is added to a number, then 6 is subtracted from the result.
6. (Large circle)   7.

8. a   9. b   10. d
11. a   12. d   13. $e = 6$
14. $f = 4$ 15. 37 seashells
16. 27 toy cars   17. 12
18. In order from left to right:
    round, round, star, round
19. Missing from the table: 7, 2, 5, 6. Rule: Divide the input by 7 to get the output.
20. Missing from the table: 50, 54, 66, 71. Rule: Subtract 9 from the input to get the output.
21. The number is doubled, halved, then is increased by a total of 4 (adding 8 and subtracting 4). The result must be 4 more than the original number.

Solid Figures, Page 94

Solid	Faces	Edges	Vertices
Cube	6	12	8
Rect. prism	6	12	8
Pyramid	5	8	5
Tri. pyramid	4	6	4
Tri. prism	5	9	6
Hex. prism	8	18	12

1. The sum of the faces and the vertices is two more than the number of edges.
2. Triangular pyramid   3. Cube
4. Rectangular prism
5. Questions and answers will vary.

Match Up, Page 95

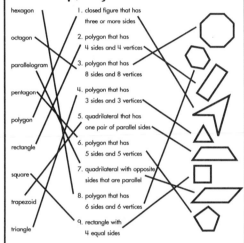

Note: More than one correct answer is possible for some definitions.

Dimensions, Page 96
1. triangle, circle   2. square, triangle
3. rectangle   4. circle, rectangle
5. 2 squares, 4 rectangles
6. 2 triangles, 3 rectangles
7. 2 hexagons, 6 rectangles   8. circle

Congruent or Similar?, Page 97
1. yellow, blue, blue
2. red, yellow, blue
3. blue, red, yellow
4. yellow, blue, red
5. red, yellow, blue

Symmetry, Page 98
1. yes   2. no   3. yes   4. no
5.–7. Check students' work.
8. DECK
9. TOM
10. MAYA
11. Students' words will vary.

Around the Rim, Page 99
1. 70 in.   2. 36 m   3. 52 cm
4. 128 yd.   5. 84 ft.   6. 32 cm
7. 66 m   8. 120 in.

Calculating Area, Page 100
1. area: 36 square units; perimeter: 26 units
2. area: 50 square units; perimeter: 30 units
3. area: 48 square units; perimeter: 28 units
4. area: 36 square units; perimeter: 30 units
5. area: 49 square units; perimeter: 28 units
6. area: 80 square units; perimeter: 36 units
7. 32 square inches
8. 30 square inches

Reflection and Rotation, Page 101
1. rotation   2. reflection
3. reflection   4. rotation
5. rotation   6. reflection

Assessment—Geometry, Pages 102–104
1. a   2. c   3. a   4. c
5. d   6. d   7. c
8. triangular pyramid   9. cylinder
10. Side R's length is 8 inches.
11. 20 square units
12. 6 faces; 8 edges; 12 vertices
13. turn or rotation   14. trapezoid
15. The perimeter of the figure is 40 cm, because all of the sides of a square are the same measure. Since there are 4 sides, the perimeter is 4 x 10 or 40 cm.
16. A congruent figure is one that is the same size and shape. A similar figure is the same shape, but may not be the same size.
17. A rhombus is a four-sided polygon with 4 sides the same length. It is different from a square because its opposite angles are congruent to each other but are not all congruent. A square's angles are all 90°.
18. The area of the figure is 35 square inches, because the length is 7 inches and the width is 5 inches. To find the area, multiply length times width. The product is 35 inches, so the area is 35 square inches.
19. A rotated figure can look the same as a reflected figure if it is rotated exactly 180°.

Customary Units of Length, Page 110
1. 21 feet   2. 2 feet
3. 2 yards   4. 52,800 feet
5. 5 feet   6. 10 yards
7. 62 inches   8. 36 inches
9. 40 inches   10. 2,640 feet
11. 2 feet   12. 1 yard
13. 12 feet   14. 1 yard
15. 39 inches

143

0-7682-2933-2 *Getting Ready to Teach Math for the New Teacher*

Answer Key

Metric Units of Length, Page 111
1. 340 mm 2. yes 3. 300 cm
4. no 5. 5,000 m 6. 10 km

Customary Units of Length, Page 112
1. 9 quarts 2. 56 pints
3. 20 cups 4. 4.5 quarts
5. 12 teaspoons 6. 6 gallons
7. 80 fluid oz. 8. 32 fluid oz.
9. 32 tablespoons
10. 10 cups in 5 days,
    not enough to fill a gallon
11. 80 drops

Selecting Appropriate Units of Capacity, Page 113
1. kL 2. kL 3. mL 4. L
5. mL 6. kL 7. mL 8. L
9. L 10. L 11. mL 12. L

Customary Units of Weight, Page 114
1. 32 oz. 2. 2.5 t. 3. 10 lbs.
4. 12,000 lbs. 5. 240 oz. 6. 320 oz.
7. 8 t. 8. 4 lbs. 9. 160 oz.
10. 32 oz. 11. 1.5 t. 12. no
13. yes

Selecting Appropriate Units of Mass, Page 115
1. g 2. kg 3. kg 4. g
5. g 6. g 7. g 8. g
9. kg 10. kg 11. g 12. kg

Brrrr, It's Cold!, Page 116
1. 70°F; 22°C 2. 32°F; 0°C
3. 90°F; 32°C 4. 50°F; 10°C
5. 15°F; −10°C 6. 60°F; 15°C

A Timely Riddle, Page 117
C. 11:09 E. 8:42 F. 10:23 H. 9:02
I. 3:21 K. 3:58 L. 2:34 M. 4:13
O. 6.48 S. 4:20 T. 12:12 X. 9:39
What time is it when the clock strikes 13?
TIME TO FIX THE CLOCK

Assessment—Measurement, Pages 118–120
1. c 2. b 3. b 4. c
5. c 6. 5 inches
7. Two pounds is equal to 32 ounces, and
   32 is 3 more than 29. The box weighs
   3 ounces more than the bag.
8. Randy is 51 inches tall.
9. c 10. c 11. d
12. a 13. d 14. 9 cm
15. 300 cm 16. 2,000 g 17. 10:26

18. Yes; Three thousand feet is equivalent
    to about 1,000 yards or a little more
    than a half mile, which is a reasonable
    distance to jog.
19. The punch will not fit into the bowl,
    because 4 liters is equivalent to 4,000
    milliliters and that is greater than the
    3,500 milliliters that the punch bowl holds.
20. Cathy should wear a short-sleeved shirt. A
    temperature of 29°C is over 80°F, which
    is weather suitable for short-sleeved shirts.
21. The baseball coach should fill the
    5-liter container with water and pour it
    into the cooler. Then she should fill the
    5-liter container with water and pour it
    into the 3-liter container. The 2 liters
    remaining can be poured into the cooler
    for a total of 7 liters.
22. The drama club rehearses for 7 hours.
    Students' explanations will vary.

What's in a Name?, Page 127
1. 5 students 2. 15 students
3. 10 students 4. 5 letters
5. 70 students 6. 5 students
7. Another five symbols would be added to
   the "3 or fewer letters" category, bringing
   the total amount to 30 students.
8. Questions and answers will vary.

Be a Sport, Page 128
1. football 2. swimming
3. 2 more students 4. karate and baseball
5. soccer; 14 students
6. 6 students 7. Answers will vary.

Line Plots, Page 129
1. 4 2. 6 3. 13 4. 28
5. yes; No students visited the media
   center 2 times during the month.
6. $\frac{1}{4}$ 7. 4 8. Questions will vary.

Line Graphs, Page 130
1. 6 miles 2. 24 miles 3. Week 2
4. Week 3 5. 168 miles 6. 18 miles
7. 21 miles 8. Accept reasonable answers.
9. Questions will vary.

Median, Mode, and Range, Page 131
1. median = 15; mode = 14; range = 8
2. median = 53; mode = 52; range = 10
3. median = 12; mode = 14; range = 9
4. median = 82; mode = 82; range = 11
5. median = 73; mode = 73; range = 8

6. median = 4; mode = 4; range = 7
7. median = 34; mode = 36; range = 5
8. median = 25; mode = 25; range = 27

Take a Chance, Page 132
1. 1: 1 out of 2; 2: 1 out of 2
2. 1: 1 out of 3; 2: 1 out of 3
3. 1: 1 out of 4; 2: 1 out of 4
4. 1: 1 out of 6; 2: 1 out of 6
5. 1: 1 out of 3; 2: 2 out of 3
6. 1: 2 out of 4; 2: 1 out of 4
7. 1: 1 out of 5; 2: 2 out of 5
8. 1: 1 out of 6; 2: 5 out of 6
9. 1: 2 out of 4; 2: 2 out of 4

Assessment—Data Analysis and Probability, Pages 133–136
1. b 2. c 3. d 4. 15 minutes
5. Answers will vary; one part of the graph
   should increase by one.
6. a 7. b
8. The median is the middle score; the
   mode is the score that occurs the most.
9. d 10. b 11. 120 dogs and cats
12. 10 fewer people
13. Five more fish would be needed to make
    the same number of birds; there are 15 fish
    and 20 birds represented on the graph.
14. b 15. c
16. Two visits has no X's on the line plot
    because no one visited the Media Center
    exactly two times during the month.
17. c 18. a 19. b
20. 10 + 10 = 20 21. 8 − 7 = 1
22. Predictions will vary. Look for students'
    reasoning to correspond to their answer
    and make sense.
23. Questions and answers will vary. Look
    for answers to correspond to questions
    and require a knowledge of the data in
    the graph in order to answer.
24. 100 25. 94 26. 91
27. To find the mean, add the scores. The
    total is 728. Divide the total by the
    number of scores, which is 8.
    728 ÷ 8 = 91, so the mean is 91.
28. Raul should ask his teacher to use the
    mode, which is 100. It is the highest score.
29. b 30. d
31. The probability is unlikely, or 1 out of
    6, that a 2 will be spun. There are five
    1's on the spinner, and only one 2.

0-7682-2933-2 *Getting Ready to Teach Math for the New Teacher*